The Making of a Woman Cop

THE MAKING

OF A

WOMAN COP

by MARY ELLEN ABRECHT
with BARBARA LANG STERN

William Morrow and Company, Inc.
New York   1976

Printed in the United States of America.

1 2 3 4 5   80 79 78 77 76

Library of Congress Cataloging in Publication Data

Abrecht, Mary Ellen.
  The making of a woman cop.

    1. Policewoman—Washington, D.C.—Correspondence, reminiscences, etc. 2. Abrecht, Mary Ellen. I. Stern, Barbara Lang, joint author. II. Title.
HV7911.A23A34   363.2′092′4 [B]   75-23255
ISBN 0-688-02982-5

*To my parents, Mary and Don Benson,
who made me do the same chores as my
brother when we were kids. I learned my
role so well then that later, when they tried
to tell me what activities were considered
acceptable for ladies, I wasn't listening.*
                                    MARY ELLEN

———————————

To my wonderfully extended family.
                                    BARBARA

CONTENTS

All of the crimes and injuries reported in this book are true and related to the author in the manner described. Addresses where given are accurate.

Except in the case of Sergeant Abrecht's own car numbers, scout cars and cruisers have been arbitrarily designated, although numbers used are appropriate to the police districts involved. Some names and dates have been changed; some dialogue has been added; some characters are composites and not intended to portray any real persons, living or dead.

The following is a list of the names used herein which are real:

> Sgt. Gary Lorne Abrecht
> Sgt. Mary Ellen Abrecht
> Mrs. Booker
> Larry Brown
> Officer Shirley L. Brown
> Officer Gail A. Cobb
> Inspector Crooke
> The Reverend R. Joseph Dooley
> Dick Gregory
> Mr. Keenan
> Catherine Higgs Milton

James M. Murray
Pat Nixon
Richard Nixon
Winifred Thompson
Chief of Police Jerry V. Wilson

All other names are fictitious and any similarity to real names is coincidental and unintended.

The Making of a Woman Cop

1

"WHAT'S A NICE GIRL LIKE YOU . . ."

"Abrecht."

I stepped forward.

Sergeant Roper handed me a black .38 Smith and Wesson service revolver from which he had just copied the serial number. The gun felt heavy and looked like a complex piece of equipment. I had never held a revolver before, although my dad owned one. He also kept a hunting rifle which I had probably handled a couple of times but never fired.

I watched five other police rookies—four men and a woman—receive their weapons. None of us was in uniform. I was wearing a plaid skirt and pullover sweater. In height—five feet, seven inches—I was equal to two of the men, although I weighed less. I towered over the other woman, who was a petite five one.

We were assembled at the pistol range in the basement of police headquarters, where we had been taken to qualify in shooting. It was 8 A.M. on Wednesday, December 11, 1968 —our third day as sworn officers of the Washington, D.C., Metropolitan Police Department. Three months earlier, the last thing in the world I would have imagined was that I would ever become a policewoman.

* * *

"I think you'd be happier if you had a job," my husband Gary said.

"Married two weeks and you're putting me out to work?"

Gary was right, though. We had met while he was a senior at Yale and I was in my last year at Mount Holyoke College in Massachusetts. We dated for over a year, including two semesters while I took graduate courses in New York City and Gary had a teaching job in Washington, D.C. On September 7 we were married, and I moved to Washington. But I was already restless playing homemaker in our three-and-a-half-room apartment. Furthermore, some extra income would be useful. Gary was earning only $6,800 teaching Latin to sixth graders in the public school system.

"The day care center won't hire me because I'm not black. The director said she wanted me, but they're in an all-black neighborhood and their staff is too white as it is." Washington was 72 percent black.

"So much for your college degree," Gary commented.

I had majored in religion after discarding my original intention to study mathematics because I didn't have any talent for it when compared with other Mount Holyoke students. Now the question was who in Washington would hire a liberal arts college graduate with a BA in religion.

"Would you believe the Police Department?" I mentioned the possibility half-jokingly to Gary at the end of a rundown of jobs which hadn't interested me.

The very idea had come up by pure chance. In early October, after the "help wanted" newspaper ads proved fruitless, I had gone down to the U.S. Employment Service office. They maintained a library of employers classified by fields of work, and in the Social Service notebook I came across a flier advertising a recreation job for *civilians* employed by the Police Department. To this day I don't know what that job was, because when I called the number listed, nobody knew anything about the flier. However, the recruiter on the phone quickly started mentioning all the other jobs they had. I told him I was absolutely not interested in police work. "What civilian jobs do you have?" I asked.

When he said the only nonsworn positions then open were for file clerks and typists, I said he might as well tell me a little more about what policewomen did.

"Well, you don't wear a uniform," he said encouragingly. Then he read me some literature describing the work of Youth Division officers, who investigated complaints of neglected, abused or abandoned children, helped in the counseling of runaway minors, delinquent juveniles and unwed pregnant girls, and also helped process women prisoners. Policewomen did not patrol a beat, direct traffic, control riots, investigate holdups or do most of the jobs which I associated with the police.

I think what really caught my interest were the requirements for joining. While male applicants needed only a high school diploma, women had to have a four-year college degree or the equivalent, with credits in the social sciences. To my surprise the department was a potential employer asking for credentials I had. It seemed I could join the police and do social work. I grew a little curious.

Nevertheless, when I mentioned the idea to Gary, I expected him to be appalled.

"Oh?" he said. "That sounds interesting."

Briefly and rather reluctantly I summarized the information the recruiter had given me.

Gary was intrigued. He felt the job was certainly worth exploring further. In addition, the starting salary of $8,000 was more than he was earning. We discussed it for a week, and I think his curiosity, more than mine, was responsible for my taking the next step. In any event, on Saturday, October 12, Gary drove me out to a mobile recruiting van in a parking lot of the D.C. Armory to take the written police examination.

"Are you sure I want to do this?" I asked my husband.

"Why not? You aren't committing yourself to anything."

"You can say that again." I entered the van.

A nonuniformed man took my name and verified that I had come to apply for a job. He showed me into a small room where I sat down and went through the Civil Service test.

"How was it?" Gary asked an hour later as he drove me home.

"Not very interesting," I reported. "It was like those standardized tests we had in high school. Vocabulary, reading comprehension and some—what do you call them? 'Puppy is to dog as kitten is to blank.'"

"Analogies."

"Right. Anyway, I'm afraid I passed."

In the days that followed, I continued to check out other jobs. In fact, I spent November as a substitute teacher in the public school system. Meanwhile, the idea of working for the police settled into the back of my mind and became slightly less bizarre.

I think a key factor that got me into the force was the gradualness of their recruitment process. I never had to make a single big decision. I just took lots of baby steps that brought me closer. The first had been going for the written test. About two weeks later, they sent me my score: ninety-two. They also enclosed a big, fat, blue background-investigation form, saying I was to complete it and come for a medical examination and interview on a date that was another two weeks in the future.

The background-information form was a great introduction into the masculine world of the police. All of the questions were skewed to the male applicant.

"Hey, would you listen to what they want to know?" I burst in on Gary as he was correcting papers. "They want to know how many children I've fathered." Gary grinned. "And whether my wife works." Gary shook his head. "Don't shake your head. I can't put down 'No' because that implies I have a wife who doesn't work. And they don't leave room for more than one word." I skimmed the form further. "They want our neighbors' names and addresses for the previous ten years, and they want to know whether I'm making alimony or support payments." Gary returned to his students' papers, and I started writing minuscule explanations to the police.

On Tuesday, November 19, 1968, I reported at 7:15 A.M. to police headquarters for my medical exam.

"There will be a number of you taking your physicals together," an officer told those of us already present. At that point I was the only woman in the room. A couple of men glanced at me, probably wondering, as I was, how they were going to process me with the male applicants. "While we're waiting for everyone to assemble, you can fill out these forms you're going to need."

He handed out various papers. I tried to remember my childhood diseases. I noticed the card we had to take with us when we went to get our chest X-ray was stamped "male." I corrected it, supplied the requested information and waited.

Suddenly I faced squarely the misgivings I would have to overcome to join the police. When Gary and I were at college, our four years on campus began in 1963 during the peak of the civil rights movement and ended in 1967 with the free speech and antiwar movements in full swing. Riots in Watts and Detroit marked our summer vacations. We thought about the police to be sure—fire hoses, dogs, clubs and gas—but we thought of them as a group to avoid confronting, not as a group to join. Neither of us was radical, and we had never been personally involved in any violent encounters. In fact, I had had no experience at all with the police, but I was certainly influenced by the negative rhetoric around me. Then, my year of graduate study in New York City was at Union Theological Seminary, a school affiliated with Columbia University. Nineteen sixty-eight was the year of the Columbia University riots, so the police were just not the heroes of my college generation.

The other problem was that I didn't know any policewomen. My vague imaginings were of large, rough, tough women; roller derby champs; Amazons; probably lesbians. I definitely had the feeling that women on the police force were not going to be women I would enjoy.

However, among the forty or fifty of us who finally assembled for the physical exam was one other woman. She was pretty, articulate and just back from two years of service with the Peace Corps. I liked and respected her immediately. Just knowing she too was interested in the job was encouraging and helped convince me to go through with this next step.

The physical started with everybody boarding a large bus which took us to a high school in Northwest Washington, where they had a chest X-ray clinic. Then we got back on the bus and went to the Police and Fire Clinic, which at that time was located in a decrepit old building in downtown Washington. There, the rest of the physical was handled military fashion, with everyone getting their feet examined at once, then their ears, nose and throat, and so forth. Since we two women were not going to line up in our shorts with the rest of the men, we were constantly being shuffled off to the side or put ahead or at the end of the line. We were also given an internal exam.

Next, each applicant had a brief interview with one of the department psychiatrists. His main goal was to discover any major problem which would disqualify a prospective police officer, like an eagerness to shoot guns or an obvious hostility against any particular group of people. The doctor who spoke to me was a low-keyed, easygoing man. I think the most prying question he asked was, "Do you find you get extremely nervous at times?" Most of the interview was just general chitchat, and I passed.

The other woman, however, had gone into a wholly different situation. Her psychiatrist immediately started throwing at her the kinds of questions I understand are common in army psychiatric interviews. "Do you wet your bed?" "Do you have frequent nightmares which disturb you?" At one point he asked her, "Do you have thoughts you don't like?" She was fed up and replied, "Well, *I* like them but I don't know as you would." She told me he got really ticked off at her sarcasm. Then it came out that she had had a therapeutic abortion on the recommendation of two psychiatrists who were medical student friends of hers. That was the only way to get a legal abortion then, but the police doctor used the fact to temporarily reject her pending further investigation into whether she had any real psychiatric problems. And she never did join the department, because while they were checking her past history, she got another job.

My final appointment of the day was with a recruiter whose approach was to present as many unpleasant aspects of police work as possible in an effort, I think, to test my real interest in the job. Do you realize you'll be scheduled on shift work? Midnight shift? What will your husband think of that? Do you know you'll be working in tough neighborhoods, with riffraff and young punks who'll shock a nice girl like you? I noticed that the ashtray on his desk was decorated with a realistic miniature model of a revolver. A second officer in the room, upon learning I had a temporary teaching job, suggested I would be safer with the police than in the Washington public schools!

A negative interview in some ways—but the more we talked, the more I realized I was finding the prospect challenging and satisfying. Gary and I had both considered enlisting in the Peace Corps or Vista, but our marriage plans had not jibed with their assignment schedules. Here was a chance to do something active and useful while earning money and spending my time in a way almost guaranteed not to be boring. I began to really hope I would be accepted into the department.

The phone rang on Sunday afternoon, November 24, just five days later.

"This is Officer Farragut in Recruiting," said the voice after it had verified that I was Mary Ellen Abrecht. "I am happy to inform you that you have been accepted to begin work on a probationary one-year appointment as a policewoman with the Metropolitan Police Department."

"Oh!" I said.

"This appointment is conditional on satisfactory completion of the department's background investigation of you."

"I understand."

"You will receive a letter of confirmation from the department telling you when and where to report. In the meantime, will you please arrange to bring your marriage license in to headquarters?"

"I'll bring it in tomorrow," I said, utterly mystified by the request but excited to be starting this new adventure.

A couple of days later I received written confirmation of the job offer. The form letter instructed me to report to police headquarters at 7:30 A.M. on December 9, 1968, properly attired in "a shirt, tie, coat [and] belt."

Gary said, "And don't forget to shave."

Monday, December 9.

"Raise your right hands."

The six of us being sworn in raised our right hands.

"I, Mary Ellen Abrecht, do solemnly swear that I will support and defend the Constitution of the United States against all enemies, foreign and domestic; that I will bear true faith and allegiance to the same; that I take this obligation freely without any mental reservation or purpose of evasion; that I will well and faithfully discharge the duties of the office on which I am about to enter, so help me God."

We got our badges without ceremony from the Property Division. I wondered idly how I happened to be given No. 3416 and then I put my badge in my purse.

"There is never an excuse for being late to work. Your job is to plan your schedules so that you leave home early enough to be able to handle any delays you encounter en route and still report in on time. Automobile breakdowns are your problem, not the department's. . . ."

Monday and Tuesday of our first week at recruit school consisted of a tour of police headquarters and some introductory lectures. I got my first insight into the intricate structure that operates behind the scenes of a large police department.

On Wednesday we were taken to the pistol range to qualify in shooting.

"How many of you have had experience with weapons?" Sergeant Roper was in charge of our instruction at the pistol range.

The four men had shot during military training. Neither the other woman nor I had ever fired a gun.

"Well, don't worry about experience," Sergeant Roper said. "You two ladies are probably going to learn better than these men and therefore you ladies are probably going to shoot better than these men because you're going to listen to me and learn my way instead of thinking you know it all." Police talk like any military talk uses a lot of repetition for rhythm and emphasis. I wondered whether we would often be referred to as "ladies."

We were each issued a service revolver which would be ours for as long as we were on the force, or until we had reason to turn it in.

"Each of you is required to carry your weapon not only while you are on duty but at all times when you are physically within the District of Columbia," Sergeant Roper said. "When you go to a wedding, you wear your gun. When you attend church, you take your weapon. On a picnic, at a beer party, in the movies or visiting the maternity ward of a hospital, you will be armed. You will be prepared, if necessary, to identify yourself as a police officer and to enforce or aid in the enforcement of the law." Roper surveyed us. His speech had had the desired effect. The gun and the job would be something we were going to live with. I think the men were more impressed than I was, because I recognized my job as basically social work. I did wonder just how convenient it would be to always carry my gun. I supposed most of my purses were large enough. . . .

"Most of our policewomen carry their weapons in their purses"—Roper apparently could read minds—"and ladies have a tendency to put their purses down when visiting friends. If your weapon is in your pocketbook, your pocketbook better be securely on your person at all times. I say 'securely' because a couple of months ago, an off-duty policewoman was walking down the street with her gun in her purse and her purse got snatched. There was hell to pay.

"Now should you be at home relaxing or sleeping, or relaxing or sleeping but not at home"—Roper glanced deadpan at a couple of the men—"it's your responsibility to secure your weapon. If there are children in the house, your gun should be out of their reach. It should not be accessible to deliverymen or others who chance to be around and might misuse it. Some officers keep their weapons in a wall safe or locked drawer. Out of sight on a high shelf is reasonably secure. But the locked glove compartment of an automobile is *not* secure, as you know if you've looked at any statistics on larcenies from autos."

Sergeant Roper gave a detailed demonstration on how to load, unload, aim and fire a pistol. We each put on a headset of bulky gray plastic ear covers. Then we were issued bullets and given our first chance to shoot.

I was startled by the strong kick of the gun. Each time I fired, the gun bucked back, jerking my forearm upward and sending a jolt to my shoulder. This was something I had never noticed in movie westerns. And the sound was loud even through the ear covers.

In those days, we shot at bull's eyes and assumed the classical position, standing at a 45-degree angle to the target with arm outstretched. It struck me from the first as unrealistic. The men on the streets were not going to be shooting at bull's-eyes, nor, I assumed, would they stand up fully exposed to an assailant if they could help it. As it turned out, within a couple of years, silhouette figures replaced the round targets, and officers were taught to use both hands to steady the gun while in a crouching or kneeling position. Recruits even practiced night firing, outdoors under poor lighting conditions.

We shot all day Wednesday. I followed Roper's directions and, from the first, had no difficulty hitting my target. Nor was the idea of firing a gun frightening to me, because it was in the context of a class with an instructor supervising and correcting each move. Wednesday afternoon we were shown how to clean a gun. At the end of class we were told to take it home and clean it that night.

I met Gary at our apartment. We had planned to go out for a spaghetti dinner, but first we had to search for a sporting-goods store that was open and could sell me a gun-cleaning kit.

We spent two more days at the pistol range. It was exciting in a way, and I enjoyed learning this new skill. The only problem I had was that I was getting the flu and developed a sore throat and headache. But it was my first week and I wasn't about to "go sick."

By Friday, all of us except one recruit had passed the test and qualified. The top man was an excellent shot and later, when the class had expanded to almost forty, he ended up winning the marksmanship award. I had the second highest score in our group of six. The other woman was fifth, but she was a lot better than the worst man, who I thought would never make it. Five of us spent most of Friday doing doodles while he tried over and over again to qualify. He finally did. At 4 P.M. I went home, gun in purse, from my first week at rookie school and collapsed in bed with a 101-degree fever.

2

INAUGURAL

"There is *no such thing* as a routine traffic stop." The sergeant spoke slowly and ominously as he intoned the motto of police traffic instructors. "You put on your red light and pull over a car. You walk up to give them a ticket for running a red light and they've just robbed a bank and you don't know it, but they think you know it, so they whip out their guns and blow you away."

At a signal from the instructor the room went dark. A movie projector started humming, and we watched a film enactment of right and wrong techniques for making a traffic stop.

In one scene we all recognized the danger as an officer leaned inside a car to talk to the driver. Sure enough, the driver rolled up the window enough to catch the officer's head, punched him in the face, lowered the window, pushed the officer clear and gunned the car.

In another traffic stop, the officer stood carefully back from the window next to the driver's door and requested the driver's license. The driver started to acquiesce but suddenly threw the door *open*, knocking the officer aside. The driver then appeared in the car door with a gun.

There was silence from the class. None of us had anticipated the trouble. Each of us might have acted in the same way.

The film finally ended with the correct procedure. As you approached the car, you looked in the back seat to make sure nobody was waiting there to get you. You never went as far forward as the front door. You stood just behind it, requiring the driver to turn his body in an awkward position to look at you. You watched his hands and glanced at the passengers' seats and the floor for any weapons. Those were some of the precautions for situations with one person in the car. Later we would find out how to handle a traffic stop involving passengers.

The lesson was somewhat scary and made a strong impression on me. Yet I knew policewomen did not make traffic stops. At one level, this and other lessons seemed theoretical in my case.

The official thirteen-week training program had begun for Class 199B on December 23. Our original group of six had joined with others until we numbered about forty.

We met weekdays from 7:30 A.M. to 4 P.M. in long flimsy structures which had been put up in the Anacostia Naval Station as temporary buildings during World War II. Our daily work consisted of sitting in classrooms listening to sergeants lecture about everything from the legal size of wicket fences and garbage cans to the geography of the city to the elements of a murder.

About half our class was black. I was very race-conscious at first. As a newcomer to Washington, I was keenly aware of the largely black population and the fact that in supermarkets, on buses, everywhere, I was part of a minority. In the small town of South Hadley, Massachusetts, where I had grown up, there had been no resident blacks. There had been only a few at Mount Holyoke and at Seminary in New York.

So while I was intellectually liberal, in terms of practical experience I was a racist if for no other reason than ignorance.

After being in D.C. for some months, I was beginning to distinguish between a friendly black face and a hostile one. But I still had not had enough dealings with black people to identify individuals easily. Those generalizations about all black or all oriental people looking alike are true in the sense that in any racial group with which you have little familiarity, you initially see only the predominant features. You notice the person's size, skin color, facial shape, perhaps hair style. But if several people are similar in these general aspects, it is difficult to distinguish between them.

As an intellectual liberal, I hated this idea so much I could hardly admit it. Yet at training academy, I found myself having to make the most conscious efforts to tell certain of the men apart. Once when I made the mistake of calling Officer Powell, Officer Jones, I was embarrassed beyond belief.

But the problem wasn't mine alone. One officer in particular, who had clearly grown up in a black area, was always confusing me with the other white policewoman (the third female rookie was black). I was convinced this other white woman did not look anything like me. Although we had the same hair color and skin tone, none of our features was similar, and her build was quite a bit heavier. Whenever he'd call me by her name, I'd kid him on the spot, as I'd have expected to be kidded. "Now, Sam, you know I'm not Barbara. I realize all white people look alike, but I'm Mary Ellen." Sam's mistakes gave me a sense of humor about my own predicament.

Our class had been studying for less than a month when Nixon's first inauguration approached, on Monday, January 20, 1969.

"We know there are going to be demonstrations associated with this inaugural. Chances are good you won't have direct contact with any demonstrators. If you do, remember, you are professional policemen. And women." Captain Anderson paused.

For the inaugural, as for any big event requiring a substantial number of extra police, all regular schedules were being set aside. Men on their days off had to come in and report for special duty. Leaves were canceled. Double overtime shifts were set up. And the Training Division was being closed and all trainees sent out to help in some way.

"This will be your first contact as sworn officers with the public." Captain Anderson surveyed the class. We were seated in schoolroom-type chairs on which the right arm extended into a flat writing surface. Uniforms had been rushed through for the men so they could help assist in traffic details. The two other women and I were in street clothes. I had never felt less prepared for anything than what I was hearing.

"Your actions and attitudes are to be professional. You don't get angry if someone spits at you, or calls you 'pig' or hollers other obscenities. Keep your cool. Take your cue from the older officers. As recruits you're not going to be assigned to any sensitive areas. Your purpose is to substitute in outlying beats and to free experienced men to handle crowd control. Each of you will be assigned to work with a senior officer whose partner you will be replacing. This senior man will know what to do. You do what he says. There was some—uh—overreaction on the part of some of the police in Chicago during the Democratic Convention. We don't want anything like that here. If I catch any of you beating on a hippie for no reason, I'll suspend you on the spot."

I was impressed. Here was policy I could be proud to support. I had feared that in order to be accepted as a police officer, one had to condone brutality. Apparently I was wrong, and the idea of being a D.C. policewoman began to feel more comfortable to me. I wondered whether I was part of an exceptional department or whether my views of police had been distorted.

Captain Anderson left.

Instead of routine classes for the rest of Friday morning, we were shown some films prepared by a federal agency on how to deal with Communist subversive groups. They were outdated, from the McCarthy era, and depicted demonstrators being hauled down stairs, rounded up and handled roughly. One film clip included maps indicating Communist strongpoints in a prospective takeover of the United States Government.

"Don't you think it's inappropriate to show these films to a bunch of green rookies a couple of days before we're going out to handle the inaugural?" I asked my sergeant. "A lot of people could be conned into thinking that anybody who demonstrates against Nixon is a Communist subversive and deserves to get beaten up."

The sergeant raised his shoulders in a suggestion of helplessness, boredom or both. "They're standard police intelligence films. They send 'em over, we show them."

In view of Captain Anderson's talk, the department's inconsistency was clear and disturbing. It seemed an officer with feelings different from mine could also find official support.

During the afternoon we studied traffic regulations, and the subject made sense. Before we were dismissed for the weekend, the male rookies were assigned to report Monday to different districts for periphery traffic control. Since policewomen didn't wear uniforms, they couldn't have given us similar duty even if they had wanted to, because we wouldn't have been able to stop traffic. At least not with police authority. So we three women were sent to the unit where we would eventually be working after graduation: Youth Division. I was told I would probably be answering telephones while some of the senior policewomen went to the Inaugural Ball to protect Pat Nixon and other ladies. Secret Service men could not accompany females to the powder room.

"Come on, there's nothing doing here. I'll show you my old beat."

I followed Investigator Sydney Levin to his unmarked police car, or cruiser. My senior partner had been with Youth Division for about six years. He wore plainclothes, was of medium height, getting heavy around the middle, but had strong-looking shoulders. We had been waiting on call in the Youth Division office for most of the morning.

The police radio in our cruiser crackled frequently with static and messages I didn't understand. The communications were very brief, composed largely of numbers. Levin didn't seem to be paying any attention to the calls as he pointed out the sights in Southwest Washington and tried to get as close to the parade as possible. But suddenly he grabbed the mike. "Cruiser five-oh-one, by," he said.

I hadn't even heard the dispatcher call us.

"Five-oh-one, respond to central cell block."

"Five-oh-one, ten-four." Levin hung up the mike and wheeled the cruiser around.

"I thought we were ten-ninety-nine," I said.

"Nah, you blew it again, kid. You acknowledge ten-ninety-nine if you're a one-man car. If there are two in the unit, the acknowledgment is ten-four."

"Where are we going?"

"Central cell block, like the man said."

Our class had been taken through central cell block once. It was a portion of the basement of police headquarters. "Why are we going there?"

"Unless it's a surprise party for me, I expect they've got some juveniles for us to process."

"I didn't think juveniles were handled down there."

"They aren't, except if you've got a mass demonstration and don't have time to stand around sorting prisoners before you transport them."

We entered central cell block through an underground garage. The quarters were dingy and windowless, lit by fluorescent lights which gave the place an eerie feeling. Across the cement floor at one end were a number of officers, and people in cagelike cells that could be hosed down. Levin headed in the opposite direction, waving and greeting friends as he went. I followed him to an open office where a uniformed policeman sat behind a battered desk. A blond boy on a metal bridge chair watched us enter.

"Hi, Willie, what've you got?" Levin asked the officer.

"Bunch picked up burning an American flag. The kid here got caught in the middle of them. We've got another juvenile next door. They were handing out these." The officer held up a sample flier with the heading, "Stop Nixon—Stop the Big War Machine."

Levin introduced me. Then he walked over and stood in front of the boy. "What's with you, kid?"

The blond boy returned his look with wide gray eyes.

"How'd you get mixed up in this?"

"I didn't feel I could stay at home today—"

"You didn't feel you could stay at home," Levin mimicked sarcastically.

"No, sir." The boy flushed. "There was no point just watching it on TV. I felt I had to come downtown and be part of things—"

Levin exploded. "Did you have to hang around a group that was obviously headed for trouble? Did you have to see the sights so badly you wouldn't move on when you were told to? Did you *hear* somebody on a megaphone warn people to leave?"

"Yes, sir, but everyone was staying."

"So you stayed too. And now you're seeing the sights." Levin gestured around the office. "Do you *like* what you see?"

"No, sir." The kid hesitated and then added, "But it is kind of interesting."

"Oh my God," Levin groaned, "a tourist." His voice toughened. "Have you ever been arrested before?"

"No, sir."

"Well, you damn near got yourself a police record to go along with your future. That would have been a nice college reference. I suppose you want to go to college."

The kid nodded. He looked about fourteen years old.

"Then don't do dumb-ass things!" Levin bellowed at him. He pulled out a pad and pencil. "What's your name?"

The boy took a deep breath. "I don't have to tell you my name." I was startled. "I don't have to answer any questions. I know my rights." The boy paused, his attitude a mixture of excitement and pride. "What am I being arrested for, anyway?"

"For sitting in the middle of the K Street intersection."

I remembered hearing something about K Street on our cruiser's radio.

"That's a public street," said the boy. "I have a right to sit in a public street, don't I?"

"Not when it means you're obstructing other people from driving cars or walking. They have a right to pass freely through the street." The boy was listening with apparent fascination. "The technical violation if you want to know is 'Failing to move on.' Now. I think you better answer *my* questions. What's your name?"

The youngster remained silent.

"Look, kid, if you don't tell me your name, that means

automatic detention, because once a juvenile is arrested, we can only release him to a parent or guardian." Something in that remark caught the kid's interest, and Levin laid it out more fully for him. "If we don't know who you are and what your phone number is, how can we notify your parents to come down and take you home?"

"You mean I'm not going to jail?" He sounded relieved, yet a touch disappointed.

"No, we're just going to put your name on a contact form that stays at Youth Division. If there's nothing more serious on this form when you get to be eighteen, it will be destroyed."

"My name is Peter Graham."

"Date of birth?"

Peter answered that and all the other questions. Then he said, "There's just one difficulty I guess I'd better mention. My parents are on a cruise, so you can't turn me over to them. Is there a police regulation for that?"

"Who's staying with you?"

"Nobody."

"Your parents left you completely alone at age fourteen?"

"Sure. I can take care of myself."

So here was a dilemma even I understood. If we were not charging someone for court, we weren't allowed to detain him. Yet we weren't supposed to release him unless we had a parent or guardian to release him to.

"I guess I'm a technical problem on your hands," Peter said.

"I guess you are." Levin glanced at me. "We'll have to do a little fast footwork on this one." He turned back to the boy. "Do you have any relatives in the D.C. area?"

Peter shook his head. "Ohio."

"You mean there's no one you're supposed to call if an emergency comes up?"

Peter hesitated.

"I think you better consider this an emergency," Levin prodded.

It turned out that a teacher of Peter's lived in the house next to his and was supposed to check on him occasionally. Levin told me to phone the teacher and explain the situation. "Then phone Youth Division Records and double-check that they've got nothing on him. I'll go talk to the other juvenile."

I followed Levin's instructions. Peter had told us the truth. This was his first contact with the police. While we waited for his teacher, I got Peter weighed and fingerprinted. He was interested in everything that was happening. And he certainly wanted to talk.

"You know, I'm not sorry about any of this."

"Oh?"

"Mr. Gordon said if we loved our country and wanted peace, we had to *show* our opposition to Nixon."

"Who's Mr. Gordon?"

"Our leader. I think they took him to one of the cells. Are they going to keep him in jail?"

"I don't know." I stared at the boy as I realized he had not been quite as innocently caught up in the flag burning as Levin had thought.

Peter then started talking about how Nixon was going to come in and head a big war machine and escalate the Vietnam situation. As he repeated the phrases he had picked up, he grew more excited and his voice rose. "Can't you see it's much more patriotic to burn a flag than just sit home and watch the inauguration on TV?"

"I think you better hold it down," I said. "You can still get yourself into a lot of trouble. If you keep going on about this, one of the intelligence officers here is going to establish a file on you."

"Well, it's what I believe. Don't you think people should act on their moral beliefs?"

"Yes. At the right time and in the right place. Just now you're in a police station talking to a police officer."

"Are you a regular policewoman?"

"Yes."

"How come you don't have a uniform?"

"Women police officers don't wear uniforms."

"Why not?"

"They just don't."

A few minutes later Levin entered the room with Peter's teacher, who looked very uncomfortable at being in a police station.

"I don't know what your folks are going to say," he blurted when he saw Peter.

"It was a question of principle."

"Principle!" repeated his teacher. "I'd like to know what 'principle' has to do with getting yourself into a mess like this."

"How can you say that?" Peter exclaimed. "For God's sake, *you're* our *civics* teacher!"

Levin let out a snort of laughter and the civics teacher turned red.

3

OJT

My partner for the day was Pat Perkins.

Although I was still studying at the police academy, starting January 31 our class began spending every Friday out in the field for on-the-job training.

We three women rookies reported that first Friday at 7:15 A.M. to 25 K Street, Northeast, where Youth Division headquarters occupied two stories of a building not otherwise affiliated with the police. About forty men and women worked out of Youth Division on any given shift. We were taken into the roll-call room, where we sat waiting to see what would happen next. The officers, all in plainclothes except for a handful of the men, entered and took chairs, exchanging occasional comments or jokes. The atmosphere was casual yet businesslike. The room filled quickly and roll call started promptly at seven thirty.

For anyone who has been at school a lot, roll call is a good transition to the working world. If anything is like being a student, it's sitting in a classroom facing forward, listening to somebody behind a desk call attendance and give out assignments. After this was done, another sergeant read notices from a stack on his clipboard. These were items like, "Special attention requested by Mrs. Jones on ——— Street. Juveniles throwing litter into her back yard."

Then the first sergeant read the police teletype. "Homicide requests a lookout for Georgette Robinson, Negro, female, D.O.B. [date of birth] seven-fourteen-fifty-two, five feet four inches, one hundred forty pounds, red bush hair style, hangs around the area of Eighteenth Street Northwest with nickname of Reds or Red Top." A white male whose name was not known was wanted for indecent exposure and was last seen driving a Volkswagen covered with flower decals. . . . About a dozen lookouts were read in a monotonous tone. We rookies took notes because we had been told to, but there was only one item about juveniles—a ten-year-old missing boy. So to me, the majority of material was of little immediate concern.

I met Pat Perkins at 8 A.M. immediately following roll call. She was white, tall—probably five feet ten inches—and thin as a rail, with a loud, almost brassy voice and a forceful manner. Referring occasionally to a typed report, she briefed me on an assignment she had received.

A patrolman had responded to a call the previous night and found a man shot in the arm and the assailant gone from the scene. Apparently there had been a fight over money from a bet. The wounded man stated that his assailant lived in the same building, was known to be dangerous and violent and in fact had been beating his own baby prior to the fight. The assailant's wife confirmed the latter claim. A copy of the officer's report had been forwarded by his district to Youth Division, and Officer Perkins was now going out to investigate a possible child abuse at that location.

"There's no way of knowing whether the father has returned to the apartment," she observed. "We'd better get a backup unit." Suddenly I realized that in addition to the question of child abuse, the father, armed with a gun, was on the loose and possibly at home.

Perkins called for a scout car, or marked police car, with uniformed officers to meet us at the location.

On the way over she commented, "This isn't the kind of situation we go into alone. Backup help makes sense not only because women aren't really trained to handle violence, but we're not in uniform. And today we happen to be riding in an unmarked car. So we're really without any visible signs of authority."

As we slowed down in what was clearly an all-black neighborhood, the meaning of Perkins's words dawned on me. Our first job probably would have been to convince people that we were police and not just two white women in street clothes going into an all-black tenement.

I was still race-conscious. When the backup scout car arrived a minute after us and two white officers got out, I thought, "This is ridiculous." I felt as though I were part of a great white army entering this house. I wouldn't have been surprised to have doors open and a whole bunch of black people trap us and make racial slurs. I not only half-expected it but in a way I felt we deserved it. What right did four white officers have to go into this black tenement?

The right, of course, was we were police. It was pure chance that we were all white. A rare chance at that, since the department's policy was to salt-and-pepper patrol teams whenever there were enough of both races.

We started up the stairs of a neglected but not especially dirty tenement. I was carrying my gun in my pocketbook and I wondered whether my weapon could possibly be of use to me if I needed it, since it was not at all accessible.

The tenants, it quickly became obvious, were less interested in our color than our purpose. A few of them simply wanted nothing to do with the police, but after some initial confusion, a couple of people gave us directions. We found the man who had been shot. His arm was in a sling. He directed us to the apartment where his attacker lived.

When we reached the door, I stood well to one side, being very good about observing our police school training that you never stand directly in front of a door if you are on official business. Suppose you do. You may be there merely to make inquiries, but the occupant doesn't know that and may have reason to be hiding from the law. So when he says, "Who is it?" and you answer, "Police," he fires a shotgun blast right through the door. In academy, where the instructors' job was to prepare us for the most violent situations, they drilled this lesson home by telling us stories of brother officers who had been killed just this way.

As Perkins strode squarely up to the door and knocked firmly, my heart lurched, and I nearly pulled her aside. "Carelessness kills cops" was the slogan of one of our instructors.

"Yeah, what do you want?" asked a woman's voice.

Even as I braced myself for some horrible unknown, Perkins stepped casually to the side and said, "We're looking for Mrs. Rodella Jackson. I'm Police Officer Perkins from Youth Division. We've come to see about your child."

With that the door swung open and a well-built woman wearing slacks and a cardigan sweater said eagerly, "Come in." As she noticed the two uniformed officers, a fleeting hesitation showed in her face. Then she glanced at me and once more back at Pat, whom she decided to deal with.

"Come in," she repeated.

One of the patrolmen stepped forward next to Perkins's shoulder. The woman's glance flicked to him. "*He's* not here now," she said with a note of scorn, having instinctively recognized the reason for the additional manpower. Then, cutting the officers and me cold, she directed her conversation to Pat. "He's been gone since last night, and I don't know if I'll take him back because this time he went too far. Look what he did."

She led us through a living room to a shiny white crib in the corner. It was the newest and best piece of furniture in the room.

One of the policemen asked, "Is it all right if we look around, ma'am?"

"Help yourself." Her attention never strayed from the crib. She pointed. "See what he did to my baby?"

A four- or five-month-old child—a boy if one were to judge from his blue sweater—was sitting in the crib playing with a brown plush bear and an old plastic bowl. His happy, meaningless sounds made the stripelike welts across his face seem grotesquely unreal, like makeup. One raised and bluish-purple welt slanted across his left cheek just below the eye. Another ran down the same cheek and over his mouth. His bottom lip had been split by the blow. Dried dark brown blood showed in the crack.

"He beat him with his belt," Mrs. Jackson blurted. She took the bear out of her baby's right hand and pushed back the sleeve to reveal another bruise on the inside of the forearm. I tried to imagine a grown man repeatedly hitting an infant. The baby reached out to be picked up, and Pat, who had been making notes, extended her hand and let him grasp her finger. "He's a cute baby," she said, her voice suddenly gentle.

I remembered what Perkins had told me in the car coming over. Even if there was a battered child, there probably would be very little we could do because these cases usually ended up with no one interested in prosecuting the adult who had done the beating. This time, I thought, would be different.

The two policemen returned to the living room. "There's no one else here. Any need for us to stay?"

"No. Thanks very much." Perkins turned to the woman. "Mrs. Jackson, can you tell us exactly what happened?"

"I just told you." Mrs. Jackson's voice rose. "The baby wouldn't stop crying, so he beat him with his belt." Suddenly she sounded furious and agonized. "Do you understand, the man kept *on* hitting him until I screamed at him to get out. Now you got to stop him from ever doing something like this again." Her tone lowered and her words came menacingly. "You got to tell him never to raise a hand to this child as long as he lives."

Perkins asked calmly, "This happened last evening?"

"Yeah."

"Do you remember what time?"

"Nine, nine-thirty."

Perkins was making occasional notes. "I know it's not pleasant for you, but we need to know everything you remember."

"Well, I can tell you the boiler was busted, so we were cold. That's why the child was bundled up, thank the Lord. The doctor says he's got no broken bones." Mrs. Jackson turned away from the crib. "Earl wanted to go out, but he didn't have no money because he don't get paid till today. Then the baby started crying while he was watching TV. He told me to make him stop, but I couldn't. So he went over and yelled at him to shut up. For a minute he did stop. Then he started crying again and every time Earl looked at him he cried harder until Earl just pulled off his belt and hit him. Then I screamed and he went out and he hasn't been back since. I got the lady next door to carry me and the baby to the hospital."

Mrs. Jackson didn't mention the shooting.

"Do you have the belt?"

The woman shook her head. "He took it with him."

"Did he ever hit your baby before?"

"Not as bad as this time."

"We need to take a couple of photographs," Perkins said as much to me as to Mrs. Jackson. I had the camera. Youth Division officers didn't routinely carry one, but knowing we were going out for a possible battered child, Perkins had handed me a Polaroid, because a visual record was wanted whenever possible.

We took several flash photographs of the baby. It seemed unnatural to be taking pictures of a child without caring whether he came out cute or smiling, but our goal was to document the injuries. For the moment, we had to treat the baby as an object.

"They never show up as clearly . . ." Pat muttered. I realized it was probably difficult to photograph bruises on dark skin.

Mrs. Jackson watched in silence until we had finished. "What are they for?"

"They'll be recorded with our report, and then there will be a hearing. Do you know where your husband is now?"

Mrs. Jackson shook her head.

"Well, you and your husband will be notified to come down to the U.S. Attorney's office for a hearing. Charges will be—"

"Hold on a minute. We don't need no hearing."

Perkins glanced at me. "Then you don't want to press charges?"

"That means he goes to jail?"

"It might, but more probably—"

"I don't want him in no jail," Mrs. Jackson said flatly. "Somebody's got to talk to him because he won't listen to me. But I never said I wanted him arrested."

"Mrs. Jackson, do you know your husband is wanted on an ADW?"

"A what?"

"Assault with a dangerous weapon," Perkins translated the police shorthand. "He shot a man in the arm."

"That's got nothing to do with me. Besides, him and Harrison are always at it. I'm telling you, don't mix me up in no hearing or arrest."

Pat closed her notebook. "Okay, Mrs. Jackson. We'll see what we can do."

Outside I said, "My God, why wouldn't she even agree to a hearing? If she wants a scare thrown into her husband, that might do it."

"She's afraid he'll get arrested and she doesn't want that. You better learn some facts of life. Someone's got to work. Right now that someone is her husband. What good is he to her locked up? Or sitting around a courtroom, for that matter."

We left the building, which no longer seemed threatening to me. I had expected almost any degree of violence, but not this kind of inconclusive encounter. "You mean nothing's going to be done to protect that baby?" I asked.

"Sure it is. The baby will be put under the temporary protection of Juvenile Court. There'll *be* a hearing and the parents will be warned that if the baby is beaten again, they're going to lose it."

"But Mrs. Jackson said she wouldn't testify."

"But I will. We'd only need her for the U.S. Attorney to press charges against Mr. Jackson—which probably wouldn't happen anyway because this was just a belt beating and not that serious." Perkins looked at my face. "Take my word for it: this wasn't a bad case. There were no real injuries to the child. Anyway, I'll be making out a Juvenile Court referral form. When the hearing is held, the court will take the part of the child. It's going to be a little tough on Mrs. Jackson, because she's not beating the kid, but if she can't protect it, it's still going to get taken away from her and put someplace where it will be safe. The court will assign a social worker to visit a few times and check on the situation."

"And the ADW charge?"

"Depends if that other guy—Harrison—wants to press charges. He may decide not to if he and Jackson are basically friends who just had a fight. Then they may just get Jackson on illegal possession of a gun."

"How will you know how it all turns out?"

"I won't, if you mean beyond the hearing in Juvenile Court. And by then I'll be up to my ears in ten other things." Perkins smiled wryly. "Abrecht, it's not like on TV where you have an ending before the commercial. Come on," she added, "I'm hungry. Let's get lunch."

With the start of on-the-job training, Fridays became the highlight of each week. Monday mornings the instructors knew they wouldn't get any work out of us until we had a chance to talk over what had happened on OJT. Usually these sessions focused on situations that called into question something we had been taught. Since there was practically no instruction in juvenile work, the men brought up most of the problems.

For instance we were told in academy that an M.O., or someone in need of mental observation, should be taken into police custody if he was an immediate danger to himself or somebody else and transported to the hospital in an ambulance.

"Hey, Sarge," one of the rookies said one Monday, "you told us that M.O.'s have to go in an ambulance. Well, I told my partner and he told me to shut up. He said they never call an ambulance. No ambulance in the city will take an M.O. that's violent. He said you always call a police wagon. So what do we do?"

The sergeant's answer had to be an evasion, because official policy contradicted reality. "You keep in mind that you're the one that's going to be responsible if anything happens to him, so when you're in charge you better make sure he goes in an ambulance."

"But—"

"I don't want to hear your buts."

"Abrecht."

"Sir?"

"You want to skip PT this afternoon?"

I hesitated. There was a physical training period every day, with calisthenics, running and chinups. But there were no shower facilities for females, so we women felt some reluctance about working out, particularly if it was early in the day. We would just be sweaty and uncomfortable until we went home. Since PT was not required for females, sometimes policewomen were asked to skip it and do typing, paper grading or errands the instructors suggested. I hated to type.

I answered the sergeant that I was going to class.

"You sure don't look like a jock. Where'd you learn to do pushups anyway?"

I grinned and shrugged. The first day in gym class I had been able to do five. I hadn't even realized it was unusual until the two other women and several men were unable to do any.

I had always enjoyed most physical activities. I was a Girl Scout for thirteen years, starting with the Brownies in second grade, and did lots of camping and hiking.

At home I had grown up close to a brother who was a year and a half older than I. As kids we played—and sometimes fought—together. If he had a friend over and I didn't, I joined in their exploits. After my father put up a chinning bar for my brother between two trees in our yard, I would see him work out on it and naturally I tried it for myself. We had a rec room at one end of our house, and when my father would have a wrestling match with my brother, I would get in on the fun. We'd have tests of strength, seeing who could hold the other down the longest. Sometimes my sister who was three years older than I was also joined in. My other two sisters were older still, and beyond such conduct.

By the time I was in high school, this kind of roughhousing by a girl made my parents cringe. But by then, it was too late for them to successfully counsel me on "the proper role for young ladies." I didn't like and was no good at the kind of coy behavior that said you should make sure never to beat your date at bowling or pretend to be more weak and defenseless than you were.

At the police academy, toward the end of our training course our PT class began working on self-defense. We women were now attending regularly. The director of training had learned that policewomen were skipping PT, and furthermore some instructors were excusing them from other classes and even their term papers to do administrative work. He hit the ceiling and laid down a law that policewomen were to participate in everything. So the three of us were right there with the men to learn handcuffing techniques, baton (or nightstick) techniques, holds and throws and how to get out of a choke, or yoke, which is when someone grabs you around the neck from behind. The emphasis was less on brute strength than on balance, speed and catching your opponent off guard.

I had no difficulty with these practice sessions. However, I doubted I would ever be using the skills. In the first place, I was learning baton techniques when policewomen didn't even carry a nightstick. Furthermore I didn't expect to be yoked from behind by a twelve-year-old. And it had already become clear from OJT experience that in a potentially dangerous situation, Youth Division women went in with patrol reinforcements. No policewoman had ever been killed in the line of duty. What I did not understand was why we women weren't spending our time in special training for youth work, learning a little about how to counsel kids and the problems that arose from urban living. I complained to Gary that at least there should be an organized effort to acquaint us with the special agencies available in the District where we could get assistance for the people we would be helping.

Gary listened with sympathy and with the interest he had shown from the first. He was dissatisfied teaching Latin and had discussed going to law school, but as I had continued to tell him stories about my work at the academy and OJT, he had become increasingly intrigued with the Police Department. Among other things, he felt police work would be a particularly relevant background for the eventual study of law.

I, on the other hand, wondered whether I had any talent for the law. When Gary took his Law School Aptitude Test on a Saturday in mid-April, I took it with him. We both understood, however, that he was the one seriously considering attending law school.

The police academy graduation ceremony took place on

Friday, April 25. Awards were given for the best shot, best sportsman and so forth. I got a certificate giving me a free law enforcement course of monthly lectures at the University of Maryland because I had had the highest overall grade average in my section. Graduation gave us a chance to see classmates after we had all been out working for a while, because the fact was that classes had ended several weeks before the graduation ceremony. I had transferred to Youth Division and been working as an investigator there since April 4.

4

THE BAD WITH
THE GOOD

I was getting restless. I had been driving around most of the morning with my partner, Clara Reaves, just to stay out of Youth Division headquarters. The only justification for sitting in the office was if you were waiting for a typewriter (they were in short supply) or if there weren't enough cars to go around. The driving gave me good practice at learning Washington's irregular streets and the shortest routes to different addresses. But enough was enough.

Reaves was large, capable and outgoing—a tough yet good-natured officer whom I had worked with before. Although we rookies didn't have permanent partners, a few experienced policewomen did most of the training.

Finally our cruiser got a radio order to phone the office. I pulled up at a callbox and watched Reaves unlock it. When you picked up the receiver, the nearest precinct would answer, saying "Box Sixteen" or whatever. Each box had a number, and the precinct could tell by a light on its Patrol Signal System Board which box you were calling from. You asked the precinct to connect you with the main switchboard at police headquarters, and when you got the operator there, you asked for the Youth Division extension and got your message. More often than not, the voice finally talking to you sounded distant enough to be coming from China.

Reaves returned to the car and took the wheel. "They want us for a narcotics strip search. Have you done one yet?"

"No." Both the other policewomen in my class had gotten strip searches during OJT, but I'd been working a month and still hadn't had one come up.

"You'll watch me then."

Ten minutes later we pulled up behind a scout car and two unmarked cruisers which Reaves identified as belonging to Narcotics Division. We were outside a run-down transients' hotel. A uniformed officer in the scout car directed us to a room upstairs, where we found four narcotics detectives and a uniformed officer holding a male and female suspect. The officers had already searched the man. One of them pointed to the woman. "We patted her down, and she's not armed." He was holding her handbag.

"Okay, love, let's leave the boys behind." Reaves took the woman by the elbow and steered her into the bathroom. The woman, like Reaves, was black, and probably around thirty-five, although it was hard to tell because she was thin and strung-out-looking. She wore an ill-fitting blond wig. I followed them into the john and closed the door behind us.

"Well, now, it's just us girls. Let's have a look at your clothes," Reaves said.

The woman remained silent and motionless.

"Take off your dress, please."

The woman didn't move.

"One way or another, honey, we're gonna do a strip search on you. It's not my idea of fun either, but why don't you just start undressing and we'll all get out of here quicker."

The woman stepped out of her dress and handed it to Reaves, who first checked a small pocket in the blouse part and then went over the hem and seams to be sure nothing was sewn into them. The suspect stood in her underwear watching. Reaves put the dress on the closed toilet seat. "Slip?"

The woman pulled her slip down over her hips and passed it over. Reaves checked it quickly. "Next?" Reaves glanced at me. "This is a hell of a lot more work in the winter."

The woman stood motionless and skinny in her bra, panties and sandals. Reaves said, "Come on, sugar, it's ninety degrees in here anyhow. You'll be more comfortable than we are."

To me this whole scene was repellent. Yet at the same time I thought of it as a cure for some of my naiveté.

The bra Reaves checked was padded, but she found nothing in it or the panties. She examined the heels of the sandals, and they were securely attached.

"Gimme my stuff back, whore." The woman spoke for the first time.

Reaves sighed loudly. "I have a hunch you know we're not through. Anyway, I've got to ask you to turn around and squat down and use your hands to separate your cheeks."

"Go to hell."

"I'd probably have a better time there," Reaves agreed. "Now why don't you just get it over with. One quick look isn't going to hurt you or show me anything I haven't seen before."

Suddenly the woman did as Reaves had requested, except that she moved her rear around in what was clearly the most insulting, obscene fashion she could manage.

When the woman stood up Reaves said, "Okay, you can get dressed while I check your wig."

The woman backed away.

"There are five cops outside."

The woman uttered a curse and threw her wig on the floor. Her own hair was cut within a half-inch of her head.

"Watch her," Reaves told me, reaching for the wig. A minute later Reaves was ripping at a seam. She pulled out a series of cellophane bags filled with white powder. They looked just like the samples we had been shown at police academy.

In the car Reaves said, "It's worse when you go through that and don't find anything."

"I guess you get used to it."

"Maybe you don't really get used to it. You just get so you can handle it. And when you take some stuff out of circulation, you figure maybe you got a pusher. Or maybe some kid who's clean might not get turned onto it."

I nodded and started the car. "Where to?"

Reaves gave me an address where she wanted to get a signature. "Abrecht, you can't be squeamish about this," she said suddenly. "Earlier this year I made a woman take off a Kotex and she sure as hell wasn't using it for sanitary reasons. She had two strips of stuff taped into that pad that you wouldn't have believed. All she was hoping for was some dainty type policewoman who wasn't going to say, 'Hey, lady, take off your pad,' and she'd have gotten away with it."

Reaves added that she had heard stories of money and narcotics being found in a prisoner's vagina. The matrons at the Women's Detention Center wore surgical gloves to do thorough searches. Part of my job was to look closely enough so I could spot anything that indicated a female suspect had better be examined internally at a hospital or the Detention Center.

* * *

The Youth Division main room was set up something like a typing pool: a large open area with a couple of pillars, but instead of little typing tables, rows of desks. Every officer had his own desk and telephone. Typewriters were shared and in heavy demand. There was an immense amount of paperwork.

On the whole, Youth Division activities broke down into two basic kinds of cases. The most absorbing to me were those involving battered or neglected children. These were, in a sense, original cases, inasmuch as the charge was brought first to us. We then went out and sometimes spent days investigating the circumstances, determining the actions and capabilities of the parent or parents, questioning neighbors and relatives who might supply information, talking to doctors and generally doing everything we could to protect the future health and well-being of the child.

Occasionally there was no alternative to removing the baby permanently from the parents' care. I worked on one case, reported to us by neighbors of the family in question, where the infant was not abused, but it was so neglected that it was underweight to the point of near-starvation and was totally listless and unresponsive. It just lay there, half-dead, its body covered with sores and rashes. I went to court and got an order committing the infant to Children's Hospital, where it immediately began to gain weight and recover.

While the baby was in the hospital, I continued my investigation. It turned out that there was a history of mental retardation in the mother's family. The mother, a girl of about twenty, was simply unable to care for an infant. This was, in fact, the second time her baby had had to be hospitalized for similar reasons. The father no longer lived at home. I prepared the necessary court papers and later testified at the court hearing leading to the order that the infant not be returned to the natural parent after it was well enough to leave the hospital. It was to be placed in a foster home pending adoption.

There was no doubt in my mind that the decision was the only way to ensure the child's survival, much less its health. Yet I felt sad that there was no facility available where both mother and baby could be placed together, with the mother still able to attend her infant under qualified supervision. One of the final ironies about this case was that a nurse at Children's Hospital wanted to adopt the baby directly, but I heard that she was turned down because her job involved night-shift work, and she therefore was considered unsuitable.

In the second category of cases we handled, involving delinquents, the Youth Division role was much more secretarial than investigative. We generally did not become involved until a juvenile had already been taken into police custody. Then, whenever a person under eighteen years of age was accused of an offense, a Youth Division officer had to be at the hearing. This might take place at a stationhouse, at Criminal Investigations Division, Sex Squad or elsewhere. Our job was to protect the rights of the minor, essentially by assuring the presence at the hearing of a parent or guardian. We made certain that both the child and parent understood what was happening, which often meant explaining forms and procedures twice, on two levels. When we read the rights card, the parent, not the child, was presumed to have the best judgment as to whether a child should answer questions or say nothing. A minor could not waive his right to silence if the parent did not want him to.

All the information we gathered, whether it was from an original investigation into a child abuse or from a hearing with a delinquent, had to be written up on a PD 379, or Juvenile Reporting Form. If the respondent was being charged, we would have to make up a Court Complaint, or Form 380.

Often a number of co-respondents were involved. Separate Court Complaints for each of these respondents had to be prepared. Sometimes it took us hours to type up a whole set of Court Complaints—single-spaced, both sides of the page, and as few typos as possible because we had numerous carbon copies in our machines. One day, as we were finishing a batch of these reports, Thomas Mayhew, a uniformed Youth Division officer, walked into the room. He was holding a bundle carefully in both arms.

"Okay, who wants to take this baby from me?"

Everyone in the office volunteered for the assignment, and I guess my voice was the loudest. I glanced quickly at Reaves, because she was my senior partner and it really wasn't up to me to request an assignment. She grinned and nodded. I went to the front of the room and took the baby, wrapped in a white cotton blanket. "It was abandoned at the Welfare Building. I'll be right back," Mayhew said.

I held the infant in my arms while work at Youth Division halted as people stood around speculating on the baby's age, sex and heritage. It was clearly a very young infant. Mayhew returned with a carton of Pampers and a box of prepared baby formula. "The mother left these with the kid."

The rest of the officers except for Reaves returned to work. Mayhew brought over a cup of coffee, and while the child slept on my desk he told Reaves and me the story.

He had been out cruising that morning when he heard a call for a scout car to check for the abandoned baby at 122 C Street, Northwest. Since Mayhew was within a couple of blocks of the address, he had volunteered for the run.

At the Welfare Building, Mayhew found the baby being cared for by Winifred Thompson, director of the District

Social Services Administration. The building custodian had discovered the infant in a stairwell at the bottom of some outdoor steps leading to the basement. When no one could figure out whose baby it might be, Mrs. Thompson had called the newspapers, partly because here was an appealing publicity story, but also because a photograph and news coverage might help identify the infant. She had also phoned the police.

Interviewing witnesses, Mayhew found an employee who had noticed a taxi parked outside the building when she arrived at work. Mayhew phoned the cab companies and located the driver. In Washington, cab drivers are required by law to keep a log sheet of where they pick up and deliver people. The driver said he had picked up a woman and her baby at D.C. General Hospital, taken her to the Welfare Building, waited for her, and then driven her to a second address which he gave Mayhew. He had not been concerned that she had left the baby because at that Welfare address the cabby assumed she had turned it over to someone appropriate. He was also able to supply the woman's name. His company had requested it so he could identify her among the many people who might be waiting for taxis at the hospital.

Now Mayhew was leaving the baby at Youth Division headquarters while he went to look for the mother.

It was 11:30 A.M. We changed and fed the tiny boy.

By one-thirty that afternoon, Mayhew had located the mother and brought her to Youth Division. She was in her early twenties, unmarried and in a highly emotional state. She didn't want to see the baby. We took her into the sergeant's office to talk to her in privacy. She told us she did not know who the father was and she could not afford to keep the baby herself. Nor did she want help in caring for it. She wanted to put it up for adoption. While still in the hospital she had called Junior Village, a home for children, and told them she wanted to bring the baby there, but they said they couldn't take it until it was six months old. She had left the hospital intending to ask a social worker at the Welfare Building about getting the infant adopted. Then she had chickened out and just left it on the steps instead.

Reaves called the Family Division of Superior Court, and shortly after 3 P.M. we all drove over. I had the baby in my lap. The mother alternated between crying and protesting against going to the court.

In the hall outside the courtroom, we met the social worker who had been assigned to the case, and the Assistant Corporation Counsel. He is an attorney acting on behalf of the District of Columbia, which is the "corporation." Almost as soon as we started bringing them up to date, the mother became hysterical. She yelled that she had told the police everything and sobbed that she wanted to go home. Although we obviously had means to prevent her from leaving, we decided there wasn't much point to it, and she ran out of the building.

"Well, we won't have any difficulty getting this one adopted," the social worker said. "He's healthy, a brand-new baby—ideal case."

"But what happens to him now?" I was still holding him.

"The judge will probably commit him to D.C. General for care until they get a foster home set up, pending adoption."

"D.C. General! We can't let this baby get stuck away there." I had been around enough to know that D.C. General was the public hospital, and like most such institutions, it was overcrowded and understaffed. The few times I had been there on police business, it had depressed me terribly. Care was impersonal and minimal, and you just knew a healthy baby was going to lie there and be fed but not get any of the attention that all psychologists say a newborn infant needs. "Couldn't we try to get him into Children's Hospital instead?"

"Healthy abandoned children under six months old are routinely committed to D.C. General," the attorney said.

"Yeah, *healthy* abandoned children," Reaves repeated with a definite insinuation in her tone.

We all looked at each other.

"He is healthy, isn't he?" the social worker asked with real concern. Then suddenly she caught on.

"I don't suppose we can be absolutely sure how healthy any abandoned baby is," I suggested. "His mother left him on the outside steps—"

"Exposed to the elements," Reaves chimed in.

"Some elements," the attorney said. It was a warm spring day.

"But it might be worth a try," the social worker added, and the attorney didn't object.

By the time we went before the judge, we had thought things through a little further. We obscured the fact that all evidence showed this was a healthy baby, or that we knew he had been abandoned for only an hour. We left out the Pampers and baby formula and exaggerated the tragic part. The mother had abandoned her infant on some outside basement steps and who knew when she had fed him last or what kind of condition he was really in. Clearly he needed a thorough examination and probably medical care.

At 4 P.M. the judge issued an order of commitment to Children's Hospital. I couldn't tell whether he suspected what was really going on.

Reaves and I, with the baby, went directly from Juvenile Court to the U.S. Attorney's office in the neighboring building. In Juvenile Court, the baby had technically been the respondent, charged, so to speak, with being neglected. In adult court, we had to give the facts to the U.S. Attorney to get a decision from him as to whether we should prosecute the mother for abandonment, which is a crime. He decided there was no need to do this, and I felt satisfied with his conclusion. The mother had made some efforts to place her baby in responsible hands, but she was ignorant about what to do, and frightened as well.

At 5:30 P.M. Reaves and I delivered the baby to Children's Hospital.

"What have you got here?" a woman doctor greeted us in the emergency room.

Reaves and I showed her the commitment papers and said, "It's an abandoned baby. He needs to be examined and—"

The doctor had put the infant on an examining table, opened the blanket and was looking at him. "He looks okay to me. Are you sure this isn't a D.C. General case?"

Reaves and I by that time were quite proficient in presenting this situation at its worst. The doctor caught on quickly.

"Okay, we'll hold him for examination," she said. We were just leaving when we heard her call the ward. "This is Dr. Rogatz in Emergency. You've got a well baby coming up. I'm writing orders for lots of tender loving care."

5

UNDER COVER

It was difficult in a department store to get a pocketbook that had adequate provisions inside for carrying a gun. The best I had found was a bulky bag with a large enough inner compartment for my weapon, but it was unattractive and cumbersome.

I had always liked the natural-leather purses you could buy at leather shops, and I had heard that some of these shops would add special adaptations since they made the bags on the premises anyway. So one summer day I walked into a small store run by a hippie-type couple and picked out a nice brown leather shoulder purse.

"Is it possible to get special fittings inside this?" I asked the bearded young man behind the counter.

"Sure, but we'll have to charge you extra for the work."

"That's okay." I hesitated over how to present my request. "Look, don't be upset, but I'd like to ask you to put a gun holster inside this bag."

"A gun holster," he repeated, watching as I took my service revolver out of my own purse and unloaded the bullets before putting the empty gun on the counter so he could trace the size.

"You see, I'm—"

"I suppose you're afraid to be on the streets at night," he interrupted, looking at the gun and smoothing his beard. "Well, it's a sad commentary on the world we live in, but I can't blame you. Sure, we'll take care of it." And he reached for the gun.

I looked at him in disbelief. He not only hadn't been startled by my request, but he wasn't even questioning the fact that I had a gun, possibly without a permit, much less that I was asking him to stitch a concealed compartment inside my purse to hold it, which was absolutely illegal.

"Look," I said, "you might want to know that I'm allowed —in fact, I have to carry a gun because I'm a policewoman."

"You're the *fuzz?"* At that his bearded jaw actually did drop open in astonishment.

Being on the department changed the pattern of my life, but in a sense, it affected Gary even more profoundly. We had both done well on the Law School Aptitude Tests. However, in June, when his teaching semester ended, Gary joined the police force. Our family and friends were shocked.

While my joining the department had struck them as a bit unusual, most people seemed to feel I had found a good, well-paying, secure job in a social service type of field. No one suggested that I was wasting my education or that my career was in any sense below me.

The reaction to Gary's decision was entirely different. "Good heavens, what's an Ivy League college graduate doing joining the police?" Apparently more was expected of a man with a B.A. in economics from Yale than of a woman with a B.A. in religion from Mount Holyoke. Comments were made about Gary's prospects as a lawyer or corporate executive. If he was bent on service rather than earning large amounts of money, fields such as education or the ministry were considered appropriate. In fact, almost anything was more suitable than becoming a police officer.

While I was annoyed at hearing this double standard applied to our futures, I actually concurred in the general disapproval of Gary's move. I had gained a certain amount of respect for policemen, but not so much that I wanted to be married to one! Yet I loved Gary and wanted him to feel enthusiastic about his work, whatever it was.

Gary and I had become friends with one of my fellow rookies in police academy. From the first, Bob told us he found police work more satisfying than the jobs most of his Harvard classmates held, working inside commissions and foundations shuffling around reports about what ought to be done. Police were out seeing and doing more about city problems than almost anyone else he knew. If one stayed in the job long term and got promoted, there were real opportunities to influence and improve department policy, personnel and the quality of city life. Bob did warn Gary that initially he would have to play down his education. Just as college students thought of the police as pigs, policemen generally thought of college types as "pinko-Commie-fags." Certainly the owner of a college diploma had no advantage on the street over a high school graduate with common sense and quick reflexes. The only times a good education had obvious benefits were in writing reports or interpreting fine legal points. However, Bob found that in a subtle way his education provided some relief from the boredom that afflicted many of his fellow officers. Where they saw merely another family argument, he could often recognize patterns of behavior and interpersonal relationships straight out of a sociology text.

In any event Gary joined the department, and we became the neighborhood cop couple.

As a rookie on the force, my days off were those considered least desirable—Tuesday and Wednesday. I missed having weekends free, like everyone else, but day work ended at 4 P.M., so it wasn't too bad.

Every other week I was on the evening shift—four to midnight. During these tours, Gary would leave for police school before I woke up and return after I left for work. We wrote lots of notes to each other. I spent some of my free time studying. I was taking a course in psychology and planning to enroll for another in criminal law in the fall.

At first I was not assigned to the midnight shift, when Youth Division maintained only a skeleton crew of two or three people who stayed in the office except for specific calls. We had to be able to work alone by the time we got this duty, so rookies' names were put at the end of the roster.

At home, Gary and I shared the housework, which we kept to a minimum. He took the laundry to the local laundromat. I did the marketing and cooking, such as it was. We both did the cleaning.

Gary had never been the kind of man who wanted his wife in the kitchen or waiting on him. On our first date we had gone to a prom at Yale. On our second date, however, he came to visit me at Mount Holyoke, where my mother had a small apartment in town. The way I was raised, if you had guests for dinner, you made them comfortable in the living room and then went into the kitchen to get everything ready. Without even thinking, I went through the same routine with Gary. But when I excused myself to go get dinner, he looked at me. "Why do I have to stay here? Can't I help?"

"You certainly can," I said, mentally adding, "you darling creature." It had been a fine beginning and had never changed.

One of the experienced policewomen who trained me was Officer Jessie McCombs. She was about fifty years old and had joined the department in the days when Women's Bureau staff wore hats and white gloves. Jessie was certainly a dedicated officer, and she went ahead and did everything— in her own ladylike way. I was with her for a strip search. She spoke to the prostitute with complete respect and politeness, which I was afraid the woman thought was mockery. Afterward, McCombs said to me, "You always want to remember to carry Wash 'N Dries in your handbag in case you have to do one of these in a place where there's no sink to disinfect your hands when you're through."

Unfortunately a lot of McCombs's attitudes seemed hopelessly old-fashioned. I went with her to visit an unwed pregnant minor—a job I felt should be handled by the public health clinics and not the police. However, a place like Gale's Maternity Clinic would send a pink slip to Youth Division, giving a girl's name, address and age, and informing us that she had appeared at the clinic and was unmarried, pregnant and underage—that is, not yet eighteen. So we would have to interview her.

Our first purpose was to make sure it wasn't an unreported rape. Even though it was too late to prosecute, because your credibility in alleging force went way down if you waited months, the sex division detectives might be interested in the circumstances. The information might help them on another case. If it was a statutory rape, prosecution although unlikely was possible, since the issue of force was irrelevant. Statutory rape, or intercourse with anyone under sixteen, was illegal whether the girl was willing or not.

If the father was known, we advised the girl of her rights in getting help to support the child. We were prepared to outline the legal points of how and when to file a paternity suit.

The rest of the visit involved some brief general counseling. Many of the young women were ignorant about health care and diet, and we urged them to keep regular appointments at the clinic. We also advised them there was a public high school just for pregnant girls, where they could finish their education without having to return and face former classmates. This bit of middle-class supersensitivity turned out to have little relevance to the girls. Being an unwed teen-age mother held no social stigma for most of them. In fact, Gary told me that in one of the Southeast Washington junior high schools where he had taught, the girls had all brought their children to school on the last day of classes to show them off to their friends.

One of the problems about the interview I went on with Jessie was that she hardly acknowledged the pregnancy except in legal terms. Here we had a fourteen-year-old girl who was soon going to need maternity clothes, and McCombs was trying to convince her and her mother that if she was still going to "date" the father, she ought to have a chaperon! McCombs was a Roman Catholic and didn't say a word about birth control. I had asked Perkins how she handled these interviews, and she told me she always gave birth control a strong push. "But first you have to get their attention. Tell them if they keep on leaving it up to the guy, they'll spend a lot of time fat and pregnant. That usually does it." Despite McCombs's displeasure, I was forceful in recommending some form of birth control after the baby was born.

McCombs and I returned to the station to do the paperwork on the case. To me, it was terrible that this information was about to become part of the girl's police record. Her name would be put into the "Family" or noncriminal file. Under the place for "charge," it would say "Pregnant minor." Granted this information was shared only among police. Anyone else checking on the girl would be told "No record." But why should it be on file at all? If any policeman had dealings with this girl on some other matter, he would probably check her out at Youth Division, be given this information, and then he might look at her in a different light. I felt that by combining social and police work, we were violating her rights.

On the whole, though, I liked my job. And I always had stories to tell Gary. The most disturbing cases, involving badly battered children, at least made me feel I was doing something useful. Yet there was no chance of getting a swelled head. Sometimes I would feel pretty brave, walking with another woman into some terrible, tough tenement. Then we'd get inside and there would be a public health nurse sitting on the couch playing with a kid, and she'd comment that she came to that building regularly. Later I might pass her walking through the streets or waiting for the bus, just going about her business. In a sense, she was protected because the people knew her or recognized her job by the large black bag she carried and the navy-blue dress-type uniform she wore. But she went into all the worst places unarmed and without backup help readily available.

* * *

I was on the four-to-midnight shift one August afternoon when I got what turned out to be my first and only undercover police assignment. I was ordered to meet an investigator from Intelligence Division at 8 P.M. that evening. He needed a "date" as a cover for a detail he was on.

My Youth Division partner dropped me at the specified time and place, and within minutes, a man approached me. He looked a little like Dick Tracy—square chin, tight features, pursed lips and stiff neck. On a hot August evening in Washington, he was wearing a dark brown suit, a hat and carrying an umbrella.

"I'm Detective Maxwell. Are you Officer Abrecht?"

"Yes, sir."

"From now on, don't call me 'sir.' My name is Jud."

Jud looked me up and down. I was wearing a summer dress and heels. He saw my wedding ring and said, "Take off your ring and call your husband and tell him you will be late."

After I made the call, Detective Maxwell steered me to his car. "We're going to The Cellar Door," he said, naming a popular nightclub in Washington where Dick Gregory was entertaining. I listened attentively as he told me a little about his assignment. It involved surveillance of some groups who were supposed to be gathering in Washington to plan a major anti-Vietnam War demonstration later in the year. It seemed that Intelligence Division had gotten information that black radicals were going to join together with white student radicals in a plot to take over the nation's capital! Intelligence had further concluded that with Dick Gregory already in D.C. and a number of influential blacks coming to see him, this was an ideal time for them to hold their first big planning powwow.

Based on my own common sense, it sounded preposterous.

I just couldn't imagine that any group was scheming to seize Washington. But this guy was dead serious. He was also my senior in rank and experience. He told me our job was to go to The Cellar Door and see who was there, who talked to whom and who sat with whom. Thus Intelligence would be better able to evaluate the potential leading characters, powwow-wise.

We drove up to the club in our unmarked police car with the radio in the glove compartment, looking as much like police as a sergeant in uniform. Everything about Jud Maxwell, and especially his stiffness, bespoke the slick detective. Before we went into the club, we walked around the parked cars and Maxwell surreptitiously jotted down all the New York tags, or license plates.

Once we were seated, my job was to observe. But I kept trying to watch Dick Gregory, who is a very funny comedian.

"You're *supposed* to be looking around," Maxwell whispered. We were sitting at a little table, with Dick Gregory in a spotlight up on stage. Whenever Maxwell had a message to give me, he would put his arm around my shoulder and lean over and whisper in my ear as though I were his date. "Try to remember faces, so you can *recognize* them when we get back to the office and go over photographs," he whispered.

Another time he put his lips to my ear. "Look over there, there's a WFO!"

I hadn't the faintest idea what that was, and I was figuring to myself, "Is it dangerous? Does it move? What is it?" The only thing I could think of was it sounded close to some kind of UFO—unidentified flying object. But he hadn't said UFO, and I was thinking, "What could WFO *be*?"

Finally I decided I was rookie enough so I could ask. Acting like I was whispering sweet nothings back in his ear, I said, "What is a WFO?"

He pointed with one forefinger while his hand still rested on the table. "That guy over there."

Over there was a guy in a blue blazer and white bucks. He looked as out of it as we did in this nightclub atmosphere. I mean people were not wearing white bucks in 1969. Finally Maxwell spelled it out for me. WFO stood for Washington Field Office of the FBI! And as we sat, Maxwell looked around and started identifying more and more of the super-snoops of the Washington area. This audience was just *filled* with people like us looking at each other.

After the show we followed the crowd outside because Maxwell wanted to see who left with whom and what was going to happen after the regular crowd went home. So we stood in the alley in the shadows and whenever anybody moved, we had to get into an embrace to make it look like we had a reason for being there. We watched a number of people get into one big, fancy car which we followed for a while. "Get the tag number," Maxwell said. Then he tired of following the car, which wasn't doing anything strange anyway, so he let it go.

With that the evening's work was over. Maxwell suggested getting a bite in Chinatown and I agreed. I was starved, having had no dinner. We made an appointment to meet the following evening to go over the photographs that Intelligence Division had.

We spent about an hour going through notebooks of photos. One of the men we had followed was there, and two or three of the faces in the nightclub turned up. But what was most revealing to me were the pictures themselves: they were just snapshots taken at various public functions. Any demonstration or parade that had occurred, whether or not it was dangerous, had evidently been under surveillance. I recognized one person in the notebook not from The Cellar

Door but from a church Gary and I had attended. It was a very free-wheeling ministry with lots of open services. And there, in the Intelligence Division's notebook, was a picture of one of the characters I'd listened to in our church. The man just loved attention. Whenever there was a camera or an audience, he would stand in front of it. Well, he had obviously stood in front of the Intelligence Division's camera a number of times.

The minute we finished with the notebooks, I started gathering my things to leave. Maxwell suggested we go out to dinner again. I said I really had to get back to Youth Division because I had some other cases to work on that night. Besides, as far as I could tell, my contribution to this assignment was over.

"Okay, fine, let's go out to dinner tomorrow night," Maxwell said.

I had a funny feeling. "Nah, I've got to work tomorrow night, too."

"Well, when's your day off? Let's get together then."

My funny feeling became certainty, and I said no.

"What's the matter? Don't tell me it's just because you're married."

"Well, yeah, as a matter of fact."

"How long have you been married?"

"Nearly a year."

"Oh, that explains it. Well, I know from experience one day you're going to appreciate this offer, so just remember me. When you get tired of him, you just give me a call."

I wasn't angry. I just wanted to get out. The past two evenings, and particularly this conversation, seemed unreal. I didn't know what to say so I muttered, "Good-bye, Maxwell."

Maxwell's stiff neck got stiffer. "Wait till you've been on the department awhile, Abrecht. You'll be interested."

"As a matter of fact, Maxwell, I'm already involved with a policeman." I paused intentionally. "My husband joined the department a month ago." I left, closing the door quietly behind me.

6

THE LAW

By the end of 1969, I was feeling quite secure in my work. I had handled most types of situations that any Youth Division officer could expect. I had also made my share of mistakes, and learned from them.

One time I was called for a search. I went into the station where they were holding the woman and said, "Do you want me to do the full narcotics search or is it just for weapons?"

"Do the full narcotics search," the officer said.

So I took the woman into the bathroom and went through the entire strip search. Every policewoman develops her own style or approach toward this task. Mine was somewhere between the boisterousness of Clara Reaves and the formal politeness of Jessie McCombs. But as I was proceeding that day, the vibrations I got from the woman were that she was a perfectly nice lady in a situation where she didn't belong. She didn't look or act like a prostitute or a junkie or a dealer. She was horribly embarrassed yet cooperative—not even complaining as loudly as I'd have expected if she had done nothing wrong. She just blew all my stereotypes, so I was curious as to what kind of criminal she was.

When I finished the search, which turned up nothing, I took the officer aside and said, "By the way, she seems like a pleasant enough person. What have you got her for?"

"Oh, she's a traffic arrest. She's got so many parking warrants on her—"

"WHAT? You had me put that woman through a strip search for parking warrants? Are you *crazy?*"

Well, it was my fault as well as his. Most *citizens*—a term police use to designate everyone not connected with the department in either a uniformed or nonuniformed capacity—do not realize that a traffic violator is subject to arrest. For minor offenses, drivers are normally given the "courtesy of a ticket." However, this woman had such a slew of parking warrants that she was under arrest and she did have to be detained in a cell for a short time, waiting to go over to court. So the officer quite correctly wanted to make sure she didn't have any weapons. But I was furious because there was absolutely no reason why I had to put that woman through a complete narcotics search, and I chewed him out for not telling me the facts. However, I also learned never again to overlook asking the arresting officer about the surrounding circumstances.

Just as there had been no formal transition from the time I worked with a partner to when I worked alone, so there had been no ceremony when I began being assigned to take newer rookies with me on the job. Usually these junior partners were female. Police*men* who came to us had already had general patrol experience and, after a very short breaking-in period, were qualified to work alone.

Teaching the rookies was interesting and it helped me realize that I had learned quite a lot.

One time my junior partner and I went to a hearing for three teen-age girls who had been arrested for shoplifting. They were acting fresh and showing off in front of each other, making smart remarks about charging the police and the store detectives with false arrest. Although they had been found wearing some unpaid-for jewelry and carrying other stolen merchandise in a shopping bag, they had smooth alibis. Each girl said she thought one of the others had paid for the jewelry. And the girl with the shopping bag protested that she had merely been going to another department to match up an outfit.

It looked like a pretty clear-cut case to me. Based on their attitudes, I suspected this was not the first time they had been picked up. First offenders usually are scared when they are caught and start to cry when their parents find out what they have done. Sure enough, when we checked our records, we found out all three had prior police contacts.

"But how can you prove anything if they were still in the store when they were arrested?" my partner asked. "Wouldn't it have made a better case to wait until they were outside?"

"Sure, if you could be certain you'd catch them. Sometimes they cut and run the minute they hit the front doors. Or they have someone waiting in a car. In a department store, where it's assumed that you pay for each item by department, you can arrest the person for larceny the minute he leaves the particular department. Of course there's a gray area here. If one of these girls had just carried a blouse into the pants section, they wouldn't have picked her up. But she had two blouses in a shopping bag from another store. That's concealment, and it will be pretty hard to explain."

"What will happen to them?" the rookie asked.

"They'll probably be put on probation." Sometimes I felt as though half the kids in D.C. thought probation was a routine part of growing up.

* * *

Occasionally we ran into really tough kids. I was on the four-to-midnight shift with another rookie—a tall, beautiful woman who could have been a model—when we were called to the First District stationhouse. It was around 11 P.M. Two teen-age boys had just been brought in by a scout car. An alert patrolman had noticed one kid standing on the corner in front of a warehouse. Upon seeing the patrol car, the kid had whistled. The officer told his partner he thought the kid was a lookout for someone inside the warehouse. They got the kid into their car—he claimed he was waiting for a bus, but there were no bus routes along that street— and called for K-9 (the dog unit) and backup units to check inside the building.

Just as the additional help arrived, a second boy emerged, empty-handed. He approached the officers and volunteered the explanation that he and his friend had been out walking when he had noticed the door to the warehouse was open. He said he knew the neighborhood and usually the warehouse was shut up tight, so he had gone in to investigate whether everything was okay, or if someone inside might need help.

When my partner and I arrived at the station, he repeated this story to us, speaking with apparent candor and great politeness. He admitted that what he had done was probably foolish, but he said he certainly hoped we didn't think it was a reason to accuse him of a crime. And he was very cooperative about giving us his name and address. We phoned to get one of his parents to come down, but there was no answer. However, the phone number checked in the directory with the last name and address he had given. He said his parents must have gone out.

My partner was obviously impressed by him. She thought he was just a very nice polite kid and she was ready to sit right down and start typing our report. I, on the other hand, got very suspicious. He was too cool. I called Youth Division Records, and there was no information whatsoever on him. Yet he wasn't shook by being arrested. When we read him his rights, he responded too calmly, as though he had heard them before. He didn't have any questions about what we were doing or what forms we were writing on, and he was providing information almost before we asked for it. I decided he must have given us someone else's name and phone number.

We went in and talked to the other boy, who had been standing on the corner. This kid was a different story. He refused to say anything at all or to sign the rights card. The track marks on his arms indicated he was an addict. He hadn't been carrying any identification, but there was a cloth emblem stuck in his pocket. It turned out to be the insignia of a local high school gang known to the police. With this plus his description as a guide, one of the District officers was able to get an identification.

"We've got to think of a way to find out that first guy's real name," I said to my partner.

We went in to the second kid whom we had now identified and addressed *him* by name. "Okay, Thomas, your friend has started talking."

Thomas jumped at the mention of his name and then immediately settled back again. "Don't shit me," he said. "Raps never gave nothin' to no pig, black or white." My partner was black, as were the two arrested boys.

I motioned my partner out of the room. The nickname Thomas had just used seemed to have no connection with the name the first boy had so willingly supplied. I called Youth Division again and asked for a check on a Negro male, about seventeen years old, known by the nickname of "Raps."

We got a call back shortly with the full name: Robert

Alan Patterson. Patterson was wanted as an escapee from the maximum security juvenile facility in Laurel, Maryland. We went in and told him we knew who he was. A precinct man who accompanied us also told him that the officers searching the warehouse had found a pile of transistor radios and two small television sets he had apparently collected and then abandoned by the door before leaving the building. Patterson said, "So you earned your pay," and quietly waited for the next proceedings.

We went back to Thomas. "Your mother is on her way in," I said.

"Fuck off." He got up and started to move around the room.

I read off his mother's correct name and telephone number. Thomas started forward and an officer in the room gave him a hard shove that sent him sprawling.

Thomas began cursing me and the officer. The door opened and another policeman came in with Thomas's mother. Thomas looked at her and everyone else in the room and started screaming. "Honky white can push us around however he wants and we're just supposed to lick—"

Thomas's mother interrupted in a strong, low voice. "Quit acting like a nigger." Occasionally I had heard blacks use this expression to each other as the ultimate insult or sign of disapproval.

Robert Alan Patterson was returned to Laurel, pending trial. By the time we could have released Thomas to his mother until a court hearing, he was coming out of his high and beginning to shake and sweat, so he had to go to D.C. General for sedation.

My partner and I returned to Youth Division. Thomas's cursing had not surprised her, but she was baffled by Patterson's unshaken cool, even after he was discovered. I explained that a lot depended on how much experience the individual had had with the police. The *really* tough guy who has been into heavy stuff—like robbery-holdup—has run into detectives who he knows can get the better of him and rough him up if he gives them a hard time. So in spite of his cool exterior, he's experienced enough to be a little scared. The last thing he wants to do is provoke the police. He will continue to plot and try to think of some way out, but he'll do it quietly.

As spring of 1970 and the end of my first year in Youth Division approached, I had a decision to make. Gary had been a uniformed officer in First District since the fall and was really digging his job, which was street patrol alone.

I, on the other hand, was a little restless in the more circumscribed domain of Youth Division. The area which fascinated me most was peripheral to my job. I found myself getting much more involved in the legal elements of the offenses than in the kids themselves. I remember debating for hours with two sergeants over a larceny case we had. A boy was found with a watch, a penknife and a couple of other things belonging to some classmates at school. It turned out that his classmates had put these belongings in the wrong gym bag by mistake. When this kid picked up his bag and found the strange items, he didn't know to whom they belonged and he kept them. The issue was, should the police charge the kid with larceny? Had he stolen by keeping what someone put in his gym bag?

I finally went to the law library and researched some old English cases that set law precedents. I concluded—and announced to the others—that the criminal question hinged on the circumstances under which the items were found. In this boy's case, it was larceny because he had found the items in a locker room where he knew all he had to do was announce in a loud voice, "I've got somebody's stuff in my gym bag. Whose watch is this?" And the true owner would clearly make himself known. On the other hand, if the boy had found the things abandoned on the street, he could scream all day and probably the person who had lost them wouldn't be around to hear. So if he kept someone's possessions under those circumstances, there was probably no larceny at all. I enjoyed solving puzzles of this kind.

I also enjoyed the people I met at court and found their interests particularly compatible with mine. I talked quite a lot with the Assistant Corporation Counsels. Most of them were men, but there was a woman in charge of the entire prosecuting staff at Juvenile Court. She was the first female lawyer I had ever met. She was steadily encouraging about my interest in law.

On April 14, 1970, Gary and I left for a week's camping trip south along the Blue Ridge Parkway. During the trip, Gary decided not to go to law school—police work interested him more—and I decided to apply. My plan was to take night courses and work during the day. It would be easier on us economically, since Gary and I were planning to buy a house in the city and we would have to carry a mortgage. More important, I wasn't certain that I would make it at law school —or that my studies would be as satisfying as I sometimes envisioned. So I wanted to keep working, but I didn't think I could handle a job with shifts during my first year of law. On August 2, I transferred from Youth Division to Personnel, where I had regular day work. At the end of the month, I started night classes at Georgetown University Law Center.

7

PATROLLING WITH POCKETBOOKS OR EQUALITY FOR WOMEN

I felt in Personnel that I had completely lost touch with all the action. During the previous year I had ridden around in a cruiser, involved in all kinds of situations. Now I was in an office working 7:30 A.M. to 4 P.M., week after week, month after month, shuffling papers.

In a sense I was grateful to learn how the Personnel Department functioned. You could really get yourself screwed in an organization if you didn't have this knowledge. But I knew I had to get out. On May 1, 1971, after nearly a year in Administrative Services, my discontent crystallized. Washington broke out in massive May Day demonstrations against the Vietnam War. The police arrested thousands. (Most of those arrests were later declared unconstitutional by the courts, which ordered eradication of arrest records.) But while most officers worked long hours on demonstration details, I was restricted to my desk, pushing papers. That day I made my final decision to leave Personnel and get back into some line function.

Law school, meantime, had proved great fun from the beginning, and I was glad it could take my mind off Personnel. The first year was devoted largely to common law cases that set precedents for whole fields of practice. I looked forward to my second year, which would begin in September. Meanwhile, on July 11, 1971, I eagerly transferred from Personnel back to Youth Division. I now felt I could handle shift work and classes, too.

Youth Division now had offices in each of the seven police districts. I was assigned to First District, where Gary patrolled.

Because of my year away, I had lost my seniority. This meant, for example, that the acting sergeant, or officer who took over when the sergeant was away, was someone who had previously been junior to me. It also put me at the bottom of the list again in choice of days off.

But the biggest change I found was a sweeping reappraisal throughout the Police Department of the role of women in policing. With women's rights groups and court decisions for equal employment opportunity adding momentum to the urgent need for more police of higher quality, the department had begun a program of greater utilization of women. As early as October of 1969, newly appointed Chief of Police Jerry V. Wilson had made all requirements for new women recruits, except weight, the same as those for men. In May of 1970, just before I had transferred to Personnel, Chief Wilson had issued guidelines for the interchangeable assignment of men and women for all positions not requiring a uniform. Women began working as investigators, vice officers, clerks, community relations officers and decoys. Without question, the department was moving in the direction of equality for women.

The crucial test of real equality revolved around whether women could handle patrol. Patrol work was the backbone of the entire police service. It meant walking the beat and riding the scout cars where you got regular assignments, known as radio runs, to go handle any one of the thousands of things that happened within the community. The patrolman was the person the public visualized when it thought of a policeman. He was the one who came when your home had been broken into, who brought back your lost child, arrested the disorderly on the corner, took over at a traffic accident. Patrol experience was automatic for almost every male officer. It was considered vital in order to acquire "street sense" and it generally was requisite for promotion or reassignment to preferred duties.

Against the wishes of most of the department, Chief Wilson intended to test women on patrol. But first he had to get them into uniform. Without uniforms, women could not work effectively. They could not be recognized as police officers either by private citizens or other police. This severely limited their participation in the department, and could result in embarrassing situations such as one I had run into my first summer on the force. I had been on my way to a call when I was pulled over by a motorman who felt he had to check out this dame hightailing it through his territory in her flowered dress, sunglasses and marked police car.

I had my ID folder out by the time he got to the car. I didn't want to embarrass him unnecessarily because I certainly wanted to encourage his investigating people who might be stealing police vehicles. He just glanced at my identification and said, "I knew we had policewomen, but you sure didn't look like one."

Plans for obtaining women's uniforms were made. Chief Wilson also created the job of Policewomen's Coordinator, in order to establish a liaison between the women and the department.

Not surprisingly, the majority of policewomen already on the department were not pushing to get onto patrol. Many of them, like me, had been attracted to the special assignments where they could use their college degrees doing social service-oriented work. Most of the women who were, in fact, fighting for patrol were those who had never been attracted to police work in the past but now wanted to be allowed to do the same duties as men because that kind of exciting job appealed to them. Of course they knew little of what it involved. Even most men did not want to stay in patrol for their entire career. It was shift work, including the worst hours, being out in all kinds of weather, doing the hardest, dirtiest jobs and getting the most complaints.

I personally felt women should have an expanded role in the department, but I was skeptical about seeing them walk a beat in uniform. I felt women were physically and psychologically unsuited for street encounters. Then, in the summer of 1971, almost immediately after my return to Youth Division, I got involved in a study being set up by the Police Foundation to analyze the present role and future possibilities of women in policing. I had met the study's director, Catherine Higgs Milton, when I was in Personnel. She requested my assignment to assist in research. Chief Wilson approved the request, and during August, I visited Dallas, Indianapolis, Miami, New York City and Philadelphia to gather material for case studies.

The experience changed me radically.

I found that policies varied from city to city as to how women were hired, trained, dressed and assigned. In no single city were policewomen doing all the same jobs as men. Very *few* of the women I saw actually performed uniformed patrol duties. But as I talked to tough, capable, even daring women who worked in Criminal Investigations divisions (including Homicide, Narcotics, Sex Offenses), Internal Affairs (where complaints against police are investigated by police), Traffic and Patrol, one thing became clear. In piecemeal fashion, some woman somewhere was doing almost every one of the duties of patrol. I returned to Washington with a heightened sensitivity to discriminations against women and wrote up my report convinced that all women should not arbitrarily be kept out of patrol work.

Late in October of 1971, I became deeply involved in one of the worst cases of child abuse I had seen during my career. A man named Pack Starkey had beaten his baby girl so severely the doctors were afraid there might be permanent mental as well as physical damage. Hospital X-rays showed evidence of healed twist injuries to both legs in the knee area. The pediatrician I spoke to said these could not have happened in any natural way, like falling from a crib. A twist was a forced thing, a wrench, done by some other human being to this baby's legs.

On October 30, I obtained a warrant for the arrest of Pack Starkey on a cruelty to children charge. I arrested him that afternoon—a Saturday—and he spent the next two nights in jail until court reopened Monday morning, when he was released pending a preliminary hearing. The infant had to remain in Children's Hospital for some time.

In the middle of this investigation, I learned that I was going to be appointed Policewomen's Coordinator. My predecessor, while ably representing the policewomen already on the department, was not doing anything to change the role of women radically. Chief Wilson, I was told, wanted action. On November 2, I was transferred out of Youth Division and reassigned to work for James M. Murray, Director of Administrative Services. Only the Starkey case went with me.

On November 8, I went to court for a preliminary hearing

on Pack Starkey. He pleaded innocent and a grand jury trial date was set for January, 1972.

On Friday, December 10, the first twenty policewomen's uniforms arrived at the Property Division. When I examined them I didn't know whether to laugh or cry. The crux of my new assignment was to get women on patrol, and here I was, looking at uniforms which included navy-blue jackets and skirts (slacks optional), high-heeled pumps, and a purse. What kind of action did they expect from a cop carrying a purse? There were no belts, no provisions for carrying equipment such as a gun, bullets, handcuffs, flashlight or nightstick except in the purse, which would have to be a valise to hold all that. It was pathetic. I immediately set about obtaining Sam Browne belts as the first step toward a uniform suitable for active street work. Meanwhile, I took one of the available uniforms for myself. The rest were rapidly distributed. Additional shipments arrived before long.

Wearing my uniform for the first time had a strong, mixed impact on me. While I was glad because it signified that we were about to become a real part of the police department, I felt self-conscious, naked and exposed. An ordinary citizen doesn't walk around with a sign across his chest stating, "I am a doctor," or "I am a third-grade schoolteacher." My privacy was gone. So was my individuality. And my vanity was badly damaged.

Trying to look "pretty" had once meant a lot to me. I had been queen of our high school senior prom. Well, you could be handsome in a uniform, but you couldn't be pretty.

To make matters worse, I didn't have time to change out of uniform before going to law school. Yet I didn't want to attend class in full uniform, so I disguised myself as best I could. The result was that I went to lectures wearing klutzy shoes with laces (which I had substituted for the unsuitable high-heeled pumps issued), a navy skirt much longer than the current fashion, and a crewneck sweater pulled over my inevitable light blue shirt. At best I looked like an unstylish English schoolgirl. One of my classmates who hadn't known me the previous semester thought I was a nun.

My preoccupation with my uniform faded as I prepared for my first meeting with Chief Wilson. He had held a press conference announcing the arrival of the uniforms and emphasizing that women could now be assigned to the entire range of police duties—including scout car, foot and scooter patrol. I drafted two proposals for easing women into patrol very gradually and a third plan to go all the way and assign women interchangeably with men as soon as they had received the necessary training.

On December 27, I approached the Chief tentatively, assuming that he, like most other police administrators, was being pressured into integrating women into the force and that he wasn't genuinely enthusiastic about risking his job on experiments. To my surprise, he vehemently urged the immediate, full-integration plan. Shortly afterward, he authorized the hiring of one hundred new policewomen for full patrol duties, and the retraining and reassignment of about sixty others for the same purpose. The program was experimental and would continue for one year, at which time an evaluation would take place.

On January 8, 1972, Officer Shirley L. Brown became the District's first female patrol officer. From that moment on, there would be no more "policewomen"—only police officers, who could be either male or female. The media gave Shirley Brown considerable coverage. We welcomed the exposure because we wanted the D.C. citizens to understand our project and we hoped it would get us recruits. Yet we felt it a burden to commence our new program in the spotlight of publicity.

By February, I was hearing of specific attempts to circumvent Chief Wilson's patrol project. The Inspector in First District had asked communications dispatchers to avoid sending female officers on serious calls. He also directed his men to alert the dispatcher when they had a female partner. Instead of using the standard acknowledgment for a two-man unit, they were to acknowledge their runs with "10-4W" if their partner was a woman. I was furious about this sabotage of the Chief's intent and requested my supervisor to complain at the Chief's staff meeting.

Less than a week later, I again went over the same Inspector's head to complain that although women had been issued slacks, he was requiring "his ladies" to wear skirts on patrol. The weather was below freezing. Upon learning of my action, the Inspector called me by phone, cursed me out (a form of communication for which he was well known) and stated that women did not look good in slacks and that because of my complaint, he would take his women off patrol entirely. He did, on February 13. At about the same time, a Deputy Chief was heard to agree that policewomen should not be allowed to wear slacks or they would become dikes.

Hostility to Chief Wilson's plan was not restricted to male officials and officers. Nor to their wives. In March, I met with the first group of women who had been given supplemental training in preparation for reassignment to patrol. No official had wanted to face them to tell them they would soon be reassigned. When they learned as much from me, they became so hostile that their training instructors had to ask me to leave until they cooled off—which they never did. Many of them had day-work schedules with weekends off—positions considered "prestige jobs" in the police world. These were the jobs male officers strove for after finishing their stint on patrol. The women resisted giving them up, especially for shift work, which caused child-care problems for some. Many commanding officers also resisted the transfer of women considered valuable in their present assignments. The department remained adamant.

March was a busy month. The Starkey case was dragging on. I was eager to have the matter resolved and wondered when it would finally come to trial. Besides attending law classes, I also studied for and took the promotional exam for sergeant. It was given once a year. To qualify, an officer had to have at least three years on the department. The promotion list, based on exam grade plus personal evaluation by superiors, would come out in July. Depending where you stood on that list, you might be promoted promptly or spend many more months as an officer.

Assuming I got promoted—around fifteen hundred people took the examination—I wondered how I would fare supervising officers on patrol. I wanted to try this new job. Furthermore, it was the only choice I had besides going back to Youth Division and giving up a promotion opportunity. And I was far too competitive for that. Yet I was keenly aware of my own lack of street experience. Publicly I was a strong advocate of the right of women to go on patrol. Privately I doubted my own abilities compared with those of others. Gary tried to reassure me without making the job sound easy.

On April 6, I had my second meeting with Chief Wilson, who seemed baffled as to why we needed it.

"Sir, I believe an order should be put out by the department detailing just what the patrol project means."

"That's not necessary," Chief Wilson objected. "I've made

it perfectly clear at all my staff meetings that women are to be treated identically and equally with men."

"Sir, some officials are finding rather creative ways of making equality unequal." I mentioned the acknowledgment mode of "10-4W."

"I don't believe it."

I told the Chief that women were sometimes assigned as third partners in a car. And I described the problem of station assignments, which had to be given to a couple of officers on every tour of duty. Women were getting that assignment about twice as often as men.

Chief Wilson was getting angry.

"Sir, an official suggested at a recent staff meeting that special 'safe' beats be created for patrolwomen."

"Okay, who was that?" Chief Wilson asked. And I had to *name* the person, because he wouldn't believe me otherwise. Chief Wilson promptly called the individual into his office and confronted him openly. The result convinced the Chief that in fact his orders were not being carried out. Shortly thereafter, Chief Wilson published a nineteen-point order which I had drafted for his signature. It corrected existing "abuses" and gave guidelines for achieving the patrol project's goal of complete interchangeability of men and women in as many areas as possible.

On Friday, April 28, 1972, Packard Starkey was convicted of cruelty to children—and given a probationary sentence. On Monday, May 1, I went to court to apply for a new warrant for Starkey, who had beaten up his common-law wife over the weekend after the trial ended. She had called to tell me of the assault. The judge issued a bench warrant. Within days, the whole case was in the hands of the patrol officer who picked Starkey up, and I knew I wouldn't hear anything further about it. I felt frustrated and generally fatigued.

I concentrated on the trip abroad which Gary and I were planning for our summer vacation. As it turned out, we were in Europe during June when we read in the *International Herald Tribune* about the Watergate burglary. Although we discussed it (a rookie-school classmate of Gary's had made one of the arrests), we never imagined its vast implications. When my thoughts were on Washington, I wondered what the police promotion list would show. I felt I had completed the major part of my work as Policewomen's Coordinator. I was ready for a change.

8

ACTING SERGEANT

"I'm sure you men have noticed the unshaven face up here —not to mention some interesting developments in the police uniform." Lieutenant Lewis glanced at me and paused for appreciative sounds from the officers assembled in front of us for roll call. I squirmed with embarrassment, annoyance and the discomfort of the handcuff case on my belt, which was digging into my back. Lieutenant Lewis continued, "This is Acting Sergeant Mary Ellen Abrecht. She will be with us for a week pending her promotion and transfer to Three D in September." Lewis surveyed the men. "You may be wondering which of you will be in Sergeant Abrecht's squad. You all just keep hoping. Squad assignments will be given out later. Meanwhile I'm going to take Sergeant Abrecht in hand myself." Pause for more appreciative sounds. Increased annoyance on my part. Afterthought from Lewis, "To show her the ropes, of course. Sergeant Abrecht."

I sat forward and read a clipboard of announcements that Lieutenant Lewis had given me.

Lieutenant Lewis was blond, well built and handsome. He had blue eyes and healthy-looking teeth. I knew I shouldn't let his innuendos bother me. They were simply his method of handling an unlikely situation: namely, sergeant-to-be Mary

Ellen Abrecht who, without street experience or knowledge of the District, was soon going to take command of one of his patrol squads and who, to top things off, was a woman. I thought it was probably a draw as to whether Lewis or I was more ill at ease about my qualifications. But I would make the most of this training week I had requested and work to overcome all but one of my handicaps.

Several days earlier I had drawn items from the Property Division that I hadn't needed in my office job. A Sam Browne belt, recently made available for women, came first. This three-inch-wide heavy-duty belt would carry the rest of the equipment I got. I turned in my two-inch "purse" gun for the standard four-inch service revolver in a holster. Female officers were no longer expected to patrol with pocketbooks. However, true to form, the department hadn't quite equalized all aspects of the uniform. Women's slacks still had no pockets. This meant patrolling in a summer uniform with two small shirt pockets in which to carry money, handkerchief and all other personal items. If you were assigned to a car, you kept a briefcase on the seat. But women riding a scooter or on foot had already found themselves inconvenienced. The issue had come to a head when a woman asked an embarrassed Assistant Chief where she could carry an extra sanitary napkin while walking a beat. He was speechless. As Policewomen's Coordinator, I had been informed of the incident, which I related to Gary. His deadpan advice was that the department begin stocking police callboxes with such supplies. The department promised to add pockets to the slacks instead. But so far it hadn't been done. In preparation for my new assignment, I had slit the side seams of my pants and sewn in homemade pockets myself.

The night before my first day as acting sergeant, Gary had come home with a bag of presents a wife could receive only from a husband who was an experienced police officer. His gifts included all the equipment which was not issued but was useful or essential on patrol. There was a whistle, and a small flashlight and blackjack that would fit in my slacks pockets. There were rubber rings to put around my nightstick so it wouldn't clang in its holder, which was just a metal ring on a leather thong hanging from the belt. And a special compact holder which carried extra bullets in two rows of three each. People with a large enough waist had room to line up the bullets on their belt cowboy style, but with all the other equipment, I didn't have space.

Gary watched me try everything on. On my right hip I had my gun, with nothing before it on the belt to block my reach. Then my handcuffs enclosed in a case. In the middle of my back was the buckle for the belt's cross-strap, which went over the shoulder when a jacket was worn, but wasn't used in the summer with just a shirt. Starting from the front and going left, I first put my bullet holder, which also had rings attached beneath for my whistle and callbox key. Then a canister of Mace and, on my left hip, my nightstick.

Gary grinned at me. "Not bad! I'll tell you what my final present is. This first time, I'll Brasso all your metal and polish your leather."

"Terrific. In that case, I'll scrounge up some dinner."

"Hold it. I'm only offering because you don't know how to do a good job. I expect you to stay and learn."

"Okay. Too bad no food tonight."

"You mean I don't get a third shot at the tuna casserole?"

"I'll give you a third shot," I warned.

Despite my military appearance, Gary didn't look threatened.

*   *   *

Lieutenant Lewis gunned the car. Tires screeched as we shot forward. Lewis smiled and grabbed the microphone. "Cruiser two-ten," he said, keeping his eyes on the traffic we were dodging.

"Cruiser two-ten," the dispatcher acknowledged.

"Two-ten responding to Eighth Street, Northwest, for the unconscious person."

"Two-ten, thirteen-oh-eight."

I hadn't heard the original run, which I assumed had been given to some scout car. Nor did I know why Lewis was racing to the address. The only thing I felt confident about was the meaning of thirteen-oh-eight, which was military time for eight minutes past one in the afternoon. At the end of every communication, the dispatcher gave the time.

Lewis swerved around a slow-moving car. "Put on the red light and siren," he ordered, assuming I knew how.

My knowledge was theoretical. I had been shown the control buttons once or twice, but in Youth Division, I had never had occasion to go Code One, or expedite, to a scene. Even now I was confused.

"Are unconscious persons Code One calls?" I asked.

"You want to get there, don't you?"

I reached for the box in which the radio and the control buttons were located.

"Just put the siren on manual," Lewis said. "We only need it at intersections."

I pushed the red light button and the switch next to it. The siren went on with a fast-building wail until it was an enveloping, deafening blast. I had hit the wrong button. There were two that put the siren on automatic—one for a yelp, the other for a wail. The control for manual was elsewhere.

Lewis yelled something I couldn't hear over the noise. I crouched in the seat fumbling with knobs. Lewis screamed louder, "For Chrissake, put it on *manual*." At that moment I turned the right knob and the siren died down. "That's better," Lewis said. "We're not supposed to be going Code One in the first place. You don't have to make it obvious to the whole city."

I still didn't know what the hurry was. It was my understanding that officers in scout cars expedited to certain scenes, but officials only did so in an emergency, which an unconscious person didn't really sound like to me.

As if in answer to my perplexity, Lewis said, "I just want to be there when you get your first unconscious who's been dead a week!" He flashed his grin and roughly wheeled the cruiser around a street-repair installation. " 'Unconscious person' is what the dispatchers generally say for a dead one," he added.

I nodded. We had all heard in training school about bodies lying in apartments, undiscovered for days. Every instructor had his "best dead one" story which he would work in whether or not it had any connection with the topic he was teaching. Apparently the experience was most unpleasant in the summer, when the warm weather speeded the action of the bacteria and produced a bloated, rotting corpse. And this had been a hot August.

Lewis said, "I want you to carry the body downstairs."

Training-academy stories frequently included details of a body exploding and showering gore over whoever was handling the lower end of the stretcher.

"Sure," I said. How else was I going to respond to his hazing?

Ahead was a red light at an intersection. "Okay, let's have some noise—and kill it once we're through," Lewis said.

I put the yelp on. Lewis slowed to nearly a stop at the red light, entered the intersection cautiously and then picked up speed as we saw traffic stopping for us.

I cut the siren.

"Ve-ry good," Lewis said. "Have you ever gone Code One?"

"No."

"Well, it's not dangerous as long as you follow the rules. You pause at stop signs and you stop at red lights and then go through." He squinted at a traffic jam ahead of us. "Hit the noise."

I put on the siren, and oncoming cars moved over so Lewis could swerve into the wrong-way traffic lane and bypass the tieup. I cut the siren again. This was exciting. I felt I was playing cops and robbers.

"In a city like this, you never get up any real speed because you're constantly starting and stopping. But the way you save time is by not having to wait for a red light to change, or by being able to go around traffic jams."

We used the siren making a turn through another red light. I thought the noise as much as the speed was responsible for my pumping adrenalin. "Intersections are the most dangerous," Lewis said. "Particularly when you get near the scene of a serious crime and there are several police cars racing there at the same time. You have some pretty terrible accidents with police vehicles cracking into each other."

I hoped Lewis was watching what he was doing while he talked. His running commentary was a cram course in patrol work, and I appreciated his efforts. This was the closest I would ever come to being trained by a senior partner, a routine experience for all male and all new female patrol officers.

Lewis had started his instruction that morning, showing

me the six sectors that constituted Third District and trying
for hours to find an exciting call to take me to. But until
now, it had been a quiet, routine tour. The main thing that
had seemed to bother him was the friendly curiosity with
which I was greeted. There were waves and nodding smiles.
Once when we got out of the car to stretch our legs, a woman
holding a small child by the hand had pointed and said,
"Look at the policelady. See," she added with a kind of
reasonable lack of sense, "now ladies can be policemen too."
I certainly hadn't expected this reception, and it seemed to
drive Lewis a little crazy.

"You're not getting a real picture," he kept saying. "Take
my word for it, everybody out here doesn't love you."

Now I found myself hoping more for his sake than mine
that something serious was about to turn up.

For a minute we drove through relatively traffic-free streets.
I realized I didn't know how I was going to react to whatever
we found, so I told myself I wasn't going to react at *all*. I was
going to the scene with an experienced official and I would
damn well manage to keep my cool and not make a fool of
myself.

As we turned into Eighth Street, Northwest, we saw two
officers jump out of a scout car a block in front of us.

"We nearly beat them here," Lewis observed with satisfaction, accelerating again. "Nine times out of ten they get
to the scene well ahead of you because they're patrolling a
smaller area than the officials. And the dispatcher always sends
the closest car on a run."

I remembered my visit to the new Communications Center
in downtown Washington. All 911 emergency calls were received in its dispatch headquarters, and all calls directed to
police were sent from there. Large maps on the walls showed
the city, the boundaries of the seven police districts and the

boundaries of all the individual beats. A sophisticated system of lights and numbers indicated the location of every car and whether it was in service and available for a call or already on an assignment. A glance at the color-coded lights could even tell the dispatcher things such as which cars were equipped with jumper cables for assisting vehicles stalled in traffic or whether a particular car had a wire mesh between the front and rear seats, meaning it could be utilized as a transport vehicle for prisoners.

We braked hard on Eighth Street behind the parked scout car. "If there is a death, they'll have to have an official on the scene anyhow," Lewis said, "but the way things have been running today, we've probably got nothing more than a 'man down.' Just a drunk or heart attack." Anticipated disappointment was clear in his voice.

I followed him out of the cruiser, glancing quickly around the dismal area. A closed, warehouse-type building on the corner was bordered by a trash-filled yard and what appeared to be a parking lot for abandoned cars and partially stripped wrecks. Lewis headed through the weeds and debris with me on his heels. At the back of the parking lot we came to a doorless garage. Just inside, the two officers, one kneeling, were looking at a man lying on an old, dirty mattress. The smell of urine, garbage and filth was strong.

"He's dead," said the kneeling officer to Lewis. "Not long, from what I can tell." He got up, brushing off his knee.

I looked at the first dead body I had ever seen outside a casket. A dull, darkish-gray color seemed to have supplanted what would normally have been brown skin. It was in fact a dead color, whereas tones of brown have life to them. The man's eyes were half-open, and I had to remind myself that they were unseeing before I could take the liberty of staring at his face. It was thin and bony and, cliché though it was,

peaceful. Eyes half-open but world shut out. I couldn't estimate his age. He looked a little over forty, but I had seen
similar sad, ill-fed degenerates who turned out to be years
younger than I had guessed.

"He's a wino." I heard the officer's voice. "Lived here
awhile. In fact, I had to send him to D.C. General around last
New Year's. He was out cold—exposure and booze. I thought
he'd bought it."

I tried to imagine someone surviving the winter in this
open garage with trash-can fires. Had he been a small man,
I wondered, or did death have a miniaturizing effect? Perhaps because he was lying down, I was unable to estimate his
height or weight.

"Okay." Lewis's voice broke into my thoughts. "You've
been introduced. Now call Homicide."

I stood realizing that my reaction to my first body had been
more scientific, even curious, than emotional. It was the pity
of this man's life that had moved me. Nothing about the corpse
itself was frightening. I said to myself, "I wonder how long
they have to be dead before they get that smell everyone
talks about."

"Abrecht," Lewis said. "Homicide."

"Right."

I headed back to our cruiser at a jog. This was the first
time I had had occasion to request Homicide to respond to a
scene. I determined to be businesslike.

I sat in the driver's seat with the door open, baking in the
sun and holding the microphone. The radio was busily emit-
ting static and bursts of messages filled with numbers. On TV,
I thought, you never saw an actor-cop sitting around waiting
for a chance just to get through to the dispatcher. There was
a moment of silence and I quickly pushed the transmit button.
"Cruiser two-ten," I said into the microphone.

"Cruiser two-ten," the dispatcher acknowledged.

"Cruiser two-ten, would you send Homicide to—" Horrified, I realized I didn't have a good address to give! I made a rough estimate of where I was. "—to the twenty-three-hundred block of Eighth Street, Northwest."

"Cruiser two-ten, do you have a building or apartment number?"

Flushing hard, I replied, "Negative. Location is in a garage behind a corner warehouse."

I could hardly wait for the dispatcher to end this communication. Instead he asked, "Two-ten, is that an apparent natural?"

To myself I repeated "apparent natural?" and then realized he wanted to know whether there were signs of foul play. "That is affirmative," I answered his question.

"Two-ten, thirteen-forty-six," he signed off.

I got out of the car, ran across the street and checked a house number. My heart sank. Determinedly I returned to the car and called the dispatcher back. "On that call for Homicide, please correct the location to the twenty-two-hundred block of Eighth Street, Northwest."

"Two-ten, thirteen-forty-eight."

I returned to Lewis and the officers, who had moved away from the foul-smelling garage.

"All set?" Lewis asked.

I nodded, grateful that he apparently had not witnessed my flight across the street. "The dispatcher wanted to know if this was an apparent natural and I said yes."

"They always want to know whether it's a natural or criminal—only you don't say criminal on the air, you say 'other.' If it's a criminal, they come quicker and may send a different investigator—someone who's got time to dig into things. If it's just a question of verifying a heart attack, they'll send some detective on his way to two other things. Did you indicate this was in a garage?"

"Yes."

"Good. They'll come pretty fast, then. Most naturals take place at home in bed with a bottle of medicine on the night table. They'll want to check this out fairly thoroughly."

Lewis then introduced the officers. "I'm sure you gentlemen remember Acting Sergeant Abrecht from this morning's roll call."

Officer Bayliss smiled. "Hope this won't ruin your impression of Third District the first day you're here," he said pleasantly.

"She's finally getting the right impression," Lewis snapped.

Out on the street, a figure came around the corner of the warehouse, spotted us or the cars and turned to go back. Bayliss yelled and the figure set off at a shuffling run. Bayliss took off after him, and the figure came to a stop, apparently aware that he would never be able to outdistance the pursuing policeman.

"Come on," Lewis said to me. "You stay here and secure the scene," he told the second officer.

We half-ran to where Bayliss was questioning a watery-eyed derelict who resembled the dead man in his dirty layers of cast-off clothes and dissipated appearance. Bayliss was sweating profusely. He wiped his face and neck with a handkerchief and said to Lewis, "This is the man who called the police."

"Before you start on that," Lewis said laconically, "how about getting into proper uniform? For me, but also, there's a lady present."

Bayliss flushed, buttoned his collar and fastened his clip-on tie at the correct position.

The conversation with the derelict continued. His name

was Al, and he was a friend of the dead man's. Al had brought him some food that morning. The man was alive and seemed as well as usual. But later in the morning, when a group of these men gathered on their usual corner, the dead man hadn't shown up. Al came by the garage to check on his friend, found him lying there and couldn't rouse him, so he called the police.

"I didn't think he was dead." Al was crying. "I just thought he had to go to the hospital."

"Okay, take it easy, fella." Bayliss pulled out a pencil and note pad. "We need your name and your friend's name. Then you'll have to give a detailed statement to Homicide."

The man supplied the information. "Can I go back and—see him?"

"Yeah, go on," Bayliss said, not unkindly. "Just don't touch anything. You hear?"

"I hear," he mumbled, moving away.

Lewis said, "We better go on over, too. The guy probably died of so-called natural causes, but we've got to preserve any scene of a death for Homicide and the Medical Examiner at the morgue. They'll probably do an autopsy just to be sure he didn't die of a blow over the head from one of his wino buddies." We walked toward the garage. "You've got to watch these dead cases. You'll find times when some sentimental friend wants to go give the body a last hug and what he's really doing is just getting close enough to get into the guy's pockets or lift a watch or something. Of course old Al there already had his chance when he found the body. There's probably nothing of value left."

At the garage the dead man's friend was standing in a corner.

The detectives from Homicide arrived. Lewis briefed

them. I watched them go over the scene, impressed at the attention they gave things I wouldn't have thought were of interest. One of them poked into both trash cans and then dumped them out on the floor to go through them more carefully. The other went through an ancient valise with its top open at a peculiar angle because a back hinge was missing. They sketched the exact position of the body and poked with a long stick into all the debris and wine bottles inside the garage and around the doorway.

Lewis said, "They're looking for something that might be a weapon, or for poison or stuff like that. I don't think they're going to find anything."

Al came over. "I guess there's nobody around going to bury him proper."

"The city will take care of that."

"What happens to his stuff?"

Lewis glanced at me. "Are you a relative?" he asked Al.

There was a negative head-shake.

"Anything of value will be recorded in our property book and stored in the police property office. If it's not claimed by a relative, it goes to the city. Why? Was there something you wanted?"

"He had a picture, that's all."

"What kind of picture?"

"From the old days."

"You find any pictures in here?" Lewis asked the Homicide men.

One of them said, "Yeah, in the valise. It's framed." He came over with a photo of a man and woman, about three inches by five inches, in a scrolled metal frame. He tapped the frame. "It's probably just tin, but it could be silver that's tarnished. We better take it in."

"Sorry," Lewis said. Al shrugged and turned away. "We might as well go," Lewis said to me. "We'll meet Bayliss later so I can sign his report."

As we left, I noted that Acting Sergeant Abrecht wished the dead man's friend had gone ahead and taken the photograph when he had had the chance.

Tuesday and Wednesday with Lewis were quiet, but I steadily learned new things about the patrol routine.

Thursday afternoon Lewis was driving me along Fourteenth Street. "They're not really out in force, yet." He slowed the car to watch an occasional prostitute walking or lounging on "the Strip" where most of Washington's whoring and drug traffic took place.

"How you been, lover?" one of the large-wigged women greeted him. She kept pace with us, staring at me through the open window of the car. Suddenly she turned nasty. "Bet you don't get much sugar from that bitch."

"You better watch your mouth, Rosie, or it'll get you in trouble," Lewis called across me.

"My mouth? Honey, my mouth gets me a living." She let out a whoop of laughter. "Her mouth wouldn't help her 'cause she'd never make it out here no way."

Rosie turned her back on the car, and Lewis grinned at me. "They don't love policewomen."

"So I gather."

At the corner of Fourteenth and R streets, a man suddenly ran toward us, waving and yelling.

Lewis braked hard.

"I've been robbed," the man shouted. "They held a knife

on me and took my wallet with my money and credit cards and everything."

My side—the passenger's side—of the car was closer to the sidewalk, but the man was yelling across me at Lewis. Lewis looked at me quizzically. Eager to show I was ready, willing and able to handle the situation, I said, "Sir, when did this robbery take place?"

"Just now. Right down the street. There were two men, and one of them had a knife—"

I said to Lewis, "Should we flash a quick lookout in case a car in the area can spot the guy?"

Lewis nodded. "You call that a 'tentative.' Unlock the back door on your side and tell him to get in."

The guy described his two assailants. I got on the mike to the dispatcher. "Cruiser two-ten, a citizen just stopped us on Fourteenth and R streets. He says he's been robbed by two subjects." I described them and added that they had last been seen running south on Fourteenth Street.

The dispatcher acknowledged. Lewis said, "You don't need all those words in the beginning about a citizen stopping us. Just say 'Original tentative lookout for—' and give it."

"Okay, thanks." I turned, pencil and pad in hand, to the man in back. I took his name and address and asked, "Exactly where were you when these men accosted you?"

"Just down the street, lady. Where R comes into Fourteenth."

I made a note and was about to ask another question when Lewis suddenly interrupted. "Which place did the girl take you to?"

"What?" The subject shot him a look. I forgot the question I'd been about to ask. It had not occurred to me that this was anything more than a simple, clean robbery among strangers. I had disregarded the area we were in. "Come on, come on, where'd you meet the girl who set you up?" Lewis prodded.

The man mumbled something about a row house on R Street.

Chagrined, I picked up Lewis's line of questioning. He let me go at it for a minute and then said in a bored voice, "Okay, Abrecht, are you going to be an officer or a sergeant?"

"What do you mean?"

"Well, are you going to handle this yourself or are you going to ask the dispatcher to send you a scout car to do the work?" I gritted my teeth and I reached for the mike. "Just tell them to have a scout car meet you at this location 'cause you think you've got a robbery."

In about one minute, we were turning the subject over to two officers.

Lewis said, "A tentative lookout has to be broadcast quickly, but an official doesn't sit around and take a full report. That's not what you're being paid for. Your job is to supervise. You'll find that out in sergeant's training school." Lewis suggested I take the wheel for a while.

I turned the key in the ignition. Nothing happened. I turned it again and floored the accelerator. Still nothing except a few clicking sounds. I had a momentary feeling of mild hysteria. I couldn't even start the car right. Then I realized the battery was dead. That shouldn't have surprised me. Police cars get driven twenty-four hours a day, and the red lights, siren and radio are all a drain on the battery. Besides, we had been running the air conditioner for part of our tour, although we kept the windows open so we could hear what was going on.

"Maybe that scout can give us a boost," I said quickly. I called to one of the officers who was still standing next to his car. He said sure thing, his unit had jumper cables. His partner pulled their car nose to nose with ours. Then the officer went around to the trunk to get out the equipment.

Lewis looked at me skeptically and asked the question I had been dreading. "Do you know how to attach jumper cables?"

"No." I had seen it done but never learned myself.

Lewis shook his head silently and got out to raise the hood of our cruiser. I vowed I would get a full lesson from Gary that night. At Lewis's signal, I turned on the ignition and the engine started.

Lewis got back in the passenger's seat. "Abrecht, there are an awful lot of jobs women are really good for. I mean, even on the department, you've got Youth Division, and we always need good secretaries. This gig—well, it's lousy hours, out in all kinds of weather, dealing with miserable slobs half the time. Are you sure this is really what you want to do?"

"I'm sure," I answered grimly.

I put the car into gear, shot forward and then stepped on the brake just in time to avoid going through a red light. Lewis took a deep breath and closed his eyes.

9

FIRST WEEK—GOLD BADGE

"My God, eight hours of this and I'll go bananas," moaned the cameraman in my back seat. "We want to be realistic, but something must happen once in a while."

"I told you police work isn't like they show on TV," I countered. "Besides, we've only been out for two hours." To myself I thought, "What am I doing anyway, driving around with a camera crew in my police car—hoping for someone in my District to commit a good crime?"

It was Sunday, October 8, 1972, my first day as sergeant in Third District. I had been formally promoted and transferred to Three D on September 15. Two days before that, I had gone to the property office and collected my sergeant's stripes and badge, since I had to be in full uniform for the promotion ceremony. My new badge was gold-colored instead of silver. I was now No. S625. My yearly sergeant's pay would be $13,500. Starting pay for officers had gone up from $8,000, which was the rate when I joined the department, to $10,000. Sewing on my stripes was the most agreeable domestic chore I could remember. Gary called me "sarge" and we celebrated with an extravagant lunch out—dinner being impossible because he was working the evening shift, and we had different days off.

The promotion ceremony in the Ceremonial Courtroom of the U.S. District Courthouse had been a dress occasion and quite impressive. It was followed by two days off, preceding the start of sergeant's training school. During one of my free days, I went and requalified at the pistol range—a yearly requirement. Three weeks later, I finished sergeant's school, having been instructed in the various aspects of the supervisory role, including how to command scenes I had never been to as an officer. Mainly it was a matter of whom to notify for what, and the importance of preserving the scene. Special emphasis was placed on standing your ground, so that even if the Chief himself wanted to tromp through the spattered blood and take a look at things you wouldn't let him. I finished school feeling fairly knowledgeable in a theoretical sense. Street experience, I knew, would be another matter.

I had Saturday off, and then, since police weeks start on Sunday, I went to church in the morning and reported at 2:30 P.M. for the first day in my new job.

Even before I appeared, a camera crew was in the roll-call room setting up equipment. Lieutenant Lewis had explained to the men that a film was being made, with the department's approval, about women on patrol. So right off the bat, I was facing officers who had barely gotten to know me while I was acting sergeant, and as if it wasn't enough that they still hadn't figured me out, here I came with a camera crew. I sorely missed the chance to get started anonymously like anyone else.

At 3 P.M. following roll call, I left the station with a cameraman and sound crew (one male, one female), riding in my car. Another man in a stationwagon followed us with extra equipment.

Their comments at first mainly expressed shock at the poverty and run-down condition of the neighborhood we were driving through. Then came the questions.

"What's the number of this car?"

"Cruiser two-four-six. The cars that officials drive are called cruisers. They look just like scout, or patrol, cars, except their numbers are in a different series. All the unmarked cars that detectives drive are also called cruisers, and they have their own number sequence. Once you know the system, you can tell what kind of unit you're dealing with just by hearing its call letters."

"What's the difference between an officer and an official?"

"An officer is the rank-and-file policeman or policewoman. The term also includes detectives. An official is anyone from a sergeant up."

"How many officers are you in charge of?"

"I supervise Third Squad, which has seven officers and three scout cars assigned to it—eighty-seven, ninety-one and ninety-two."

"How do you get seven officers into three cars?"

"You don't. One might be on duty in the station or filling in for someone on sick leave or vacation. And sometimes an extra officer walks a beat."

"Are all the officers you supervise men?"

"At the moment, yes. But there is a woman in another squad in my platoon."

"What has all the stuff on the radio been?"

"I don't know. I've been so busy answering your questions I haven't had time to listen!"

They were quiet for a while and I concentrated on the dispatches. On TV shows, the police radio is as clear as any good-quality AM-FM set at home. In reality, the dispatches sometimes sound as though they're coming from the moon. On top of that, I was still so green that the messages sounded like mad jumbles of numbers with an occasional word thrown in to convince you the communication was in English. Because our tour had started at 3 P.M., even the military time, which was coming out "fifteen-oh-eight," threw me. I explained the 10-99 acknowledgment for a one-man unit, 10-4 for a two-man car, and some of the more common codes I had studied or learned while riding with Lieutenant Lewis.

"What was the dispatcher's message there? Ten-forty-six or something?"

"Darned if I know," I thought to myself. I'd been hoping they'd forget that one, because I couldn't remember what it meant. I decided I might as well find out. I pulled up, looked at the code list, and announced that 10-46 meant assist a citizen, no emergency. "It's probably something like a stalled car," I said.

"Are we going?"

"To a stalled car?" I thought. "No. Scout seventy-seven got the run and it's a Second District unit," I said. "They share our radio channel. Third District scouts start with eighty-five and go through one-oh-four."

Disappointed silence in the car.

We drove for a few minutes. I tensed once as I heard a car in my own squad come on the air, but he was asking whether the dispatcher had been advised that the traffic light at Eighteenth and Columbia was out.

Scout 69 said, "Traffic stop, Connecticut and Belmont, M Mary, N Nora, L Lincoln two zero two two."

I explained to my riders that Scout 69 had just asked for a tag, or license, check on a car he had stopped. There was a computer in the dispatching room that printed out information within seconds on any license plate of a stolen vehicle. It could also check drivers' licenses for wanted persons. It was called WALES—Washington Area Law Enforcement System.

"What made the officer stop the car in the first place?" asked one of my passengers.

"It could have been a traffic violation, or something that

looked suspicious. Maybe the car or the people in it reminded him of a lookout. Or suppose he saw shiny tags on a dirty car. If everything is on the up and up, a car and its tags should have been going the same places together. So you check it out. Maybe he just made a random stop. He doesn't need to have a reason."

We returned our attention to the radio in time to hear the dispatcher say, "Scout sixty-nine, no record on that Mary Nora Lincoln two zero two two."

A run came out for a Third District car to "investigate the trouble at the phone booth, Fifth and Elm Street, Northwest." Although it didn't sound like much, I headed in that direction. As we approached the corner and spotted the parked scout car, we heard it give its call letters and disposition, or report to the dispatcher. "Sir, boyfriend-boyfriend dispute settled at phone booth, Fifth and Elm. Subjects counseled, SOW."

"Did he say 'boyfriend-boyfriend'?" asked the woman passenger.

"Yup," I grinned, adding that SOW meant sent on their way.

Time passed slowly. Whenever someone spoke, I lost track of the radio entirely. Even concentrating, I missed a lot.

"Attention all units. Lookout for the stolen auto. Stolen auto dark brown 'Sixty-five Chevy Bel Air four-door bearing Maryland registration D David V Victor—"

I grabbed a pencil and scribbled the tag number on the top page of my clipboard. I had to start studying different makes of cars so I could recognize them readily. Male officers had an advantage here because most of them had been car-conscious from the time they were boys. We all started watching for old brown Chevies.

There was a burglar alarm call at a liquor store which quickly turned out to be false.

Cruiser 230 asked the dispatcher to have a unit respond for a man down, which meant someone hurt, drunk or sick. Since there was already an official on the scene, I ignored the call.

We continued to cruise. I felt that all kinds of things must be happening this Sunday evening and I just wasn't catching them. I picked up the microphone. "Cruiser two-four-six. Any units in Three D with reports, give me their ten-twenty."

To my surprise, one of my own cars advised the dispatcher that he had a report to be signed and gave his 10-20, or location. I acknowledged I would meet him there. He was not supposed to leave his beat.

I drove to where Scout 87 was waiting. The stationwagon with the extra equipment for the film crew pulled up behind us and its driver came over eagerly to our car. "What's up?"

Officer Rangely came to my window with a clipboard.

The sound man inside my cruiser asked, "Can you turn down your radio?"

"No," I said to him. To the stationwagon driver, "I'm just checking a report." To Rangely, a short, towheaded officer who looked like a country kid, "What have you got?"

"Larceny, bike." Rangely handed me the clipboard.

The camera started buzzing. "Ignore it," I told myself. I read Rangely's report and a wave of relief swept over me. Here was something I was familiar with. A kid had had his bike stolen that morning while he was playing with some friends. His mother had called the police. I finished the report and said to Rangely, "It doesn't sound like a larceny to me. I think you better change that to robbery."

"But the owner wasn't on the bike. It was taken off the street near him."

"Okay, it's not robbery force and violence, but pure larceny would be if the owner wasn't involved at all and the bike was just unattended. Listen to this." I read some sentences from the report describing how the bike's owner had stopped riding to talk to some friends. He had laid the bike on the ground at his feet. An older boy had grabbed it. The owner had said, "Leave my bike alone." The older boy had said, "I feel like riding." And he had pedaled away, pausing to yell back, "Hey, man, you got an awful odd-shaped ass if this seat fits you!" Rangely apparently liked accurate quotes.

Rangely conceded that he had a robbery, not larceny, and took back the report to change it.

It was getting dark when we stopped for hamburgers. We ate in our cars because the camera crew didn't want to leave their equipment, and I didn't want to leave the radio. Also, I still felt self-conscious in my uniform, particularly now that I was wearing all my equipment around my waist.

The evening continued slowly for another hour. Suddenly I heard a fire engine, saw it cross an intersection and fell in behind it. The police are called to every fire scene anyway, because they direct and coordinate the flow of traffic around the area so the firemen can concentrate on their work.

When we arrived at the scene, which was an out-of-the-way location on a little-traveled street, the camera crew leaped out of the car and started filming. I saw that the fire was relatively small, in an abandoned building that was not connected to any other structure. It turned out that a couple of winos had been sleeping in the building and left the stove on. Meantime the camera crew was grinding away while I realized I was walking around a lot to look busy, which I wasn't. None of the traditional things you learn in sergeant's school that you have to do at a fire were necessary. There weren't any cars *coming* on this back road, so I had no traffic problem. It wasn't during rush hour, so I didn't have to worry about giving a traffic broadcast to the rest of the units. There really was nothing to do, and we were gone in half an hour.

The crew said they'd gotten a lot of footage of me and the fire. "Well," I thought, "I hope they're satisfied, because that's our biggie for the day."

Monday

My passengers Sunday had been shocked by the condition of the area we were patrolling. It was real, inner city ghetto. Third District was at the center of all the precincts, surrounded on every side by other districts, the only one that didn't include any D.C. boundary. It was filled with blocks of dilapidated, sometimes partially vacant buildings, run-down stores, too many bars. Garbage, junk and litter were everywhere. On some of the blocks, to be sure, the residents were making a noticeable effort to maintain the row houses as well as they could. But the overriding impression was one of poverty, if not neglect or worse.

Toward evening the prostitutes and drug addicts came out in force, especially along the Fourteenth Street Strip. Neon lights of cheap hotels went on. As the hour grew later, the startling thing was the number of people, including young children, still on the streets.

Monday, as I drove alone for the first time, the negative impressions struck me more strongly. There were no overt acts of hostility toward me, though through my open window I heard some woman yell, "Roll on out of here, bitch." But a man who owned a fast-food store asked me if I was new on the beat and then welcomed me to the neighborhood. "Things are lookin' up around here," he said.

"Yeah, rents," commented a companion dourly.

Yet I was keenly aware of being a white person in a largely

black ghetto, of being a uniformed police official among people who had little affection for the enforcement authority they saw as representing an oppressive status quo. If I ever got in trouble in some of these neighborhoods, I didn't think anyone would call help for me, or come to my aid.

It was a quiet tour. Time crawled by slowly. I had enormous trouble with the radio. Military time drove me crazy. Then I'd listen with great attention to a call only to realize it was for Second District. Someday I would be able automatically to screen out all Two D calls by knowing its scout-car numbers. People with experience developed a knack for the radio, picking up runs assigned to them even while talking themselves. There were tales of officers who went to sleep in their scout cars and woke up when they heard their call letters.

My seat grew tired from so much sitting, and I took every opportunity to get out of the car to sign reports or talk to officers. Later in the evening a cold drizzle began to fall and things grew even slower. The weather greatly affects police work by encouraging or discouraging citizens from going outside. I wasn't bored because so many little sights and experiences that would be utterly routine to an experienced patrol officer were new to me. However, I constantly had the lost feeling that I was supposed to *be* someplace but didn't know it. I kept thinking that every other sergeant was out running helter-skelter on important matters while I just drove around calling for reports.

Checkoff time for me was 11 P.M. During each twenty-four-hour period, Third District was covered by three "sections"—day, evening and midnight. Each section was divided into two platoons, which started and finished an hour apart. Each platoon had its own set of officers, sergeants and cars. One platoon worked from three to eleven, for example; the other from four to midnight, so that all the police didn't come in off the streets at the same time when the shift changed.

Before leaving the car, I checked my mileage, which I had noted before starting out. I had driven forty-six miles during the eight uneventful hours.

I went to check off in the sergeants' room. This is a formality at the end of every tour to make sure that all officers and officials who went out are back or accounted for. A few men were standing around discussing the evening. One of the sergeants about to go on duty was saying he had heard there had been a bad stabbing over in Fourth District.

Lieutenant Lewis glanced up, spotted me and called across the room, "Hey, Abrecht, were *you* working tonight?"

Tuesday

Early in the afternoon a car in my squad got a run to check for the unconscious person behind a liquor store. I realized with a start that the address was practically around the corner from me. I grabbed the mike and told the dispatcher I was responding. A mental picture flashed through my mind of the dead wino Lieutenant Lewis and I had found when we answered the unconscious call some weeks earlier.

I drove through an alley next to the store and into a back parking lot. Because I had been so close to start with, I was first on the scene. A number of drunks were hanging around. I studied them briefly. Most seemed elderly, and I decided there was nothing about the crowd that should make me nervous. I felt that even if they wanted to start some trouble, they were too weak and disoriented to be dangerous.

When I got out of the car, one man came over to me and held out his arms, wrists tightly together. "Afternoon, ma'am."

He was weaving as he addressed me courteously. "Would you like to arrest me?" I stared and realized he was beyond the point where he could be trying to put me on. "It would be a pleasure if you'd care to take me in," he burbled.

"Not right now." I sensed that in this circumstance, my uniform was giving me some security and authority.

I could see a figure on the ground against the back wall of the parking lot. I headed for it with an eerie sense of having been through this scene before. A couple of drunks were following me curiously. I turned and called, "Please stay back." They stopped. Still no sign of another police unit.

When I reached the figure, I stared in surprise at the eyes meeting mine. This man not only wasn't dead, he was very much conscious and bleeding from a gash in his forehead.

"I fell," he said with the weak breathlessness of someone in distress. "I don't know how I fell." He seemed dazed and smelled of liquor. "My head is bleeding." His eyes closed.

"Ambulance," I thought, jumping to my feet. Even as I turned to run back to my car, I heard a siren. The dispatcher must have been given enough information to have called an ambulance immediately.

The two curious drunks wandered a little closer, and I asked if they had seen what had happened. They shook their heads.

A red D.C. ambulance rolled into the parking lot around my cruiser and pulled up just a few feet from me. The two front doors swung open and two firemen, who drive the ambulances in Washington, jumped out.

"He's got a head wound but he's conscious—or he was a minute ago," I said.

Not stopping to examine the man, they ran around behind the ambulance and returned with a stretcher. "My head is bleeding," the man said as they lifted him onto it.

"Okay, buddy, take it easy," one of the firemen said.

I leaned down. "Can you tell us your name?"

No answer. The man closed his eyes.

Some of our audience had moved closer. While the firemen loaded the stretcher, I went over and asked whether anyone knew the injured man or had seen what had happened. There were shrugs and mumbles and no real information.

One of the firemen stayed inside the ambulance to ride with the injured man. The other one slammed the double back doors shut, turned and called, "We'll take him to Freedmen's Hospital. They can talk to him there." He started for the front of the ambulance and stopped as something suddenly seemed to dawn on him. He looked at me. "What are *you* doing back here alone?"

"Same thing you are." Sometimes appropriate answers came to me when needed instead of two hours late.

Wednesday

I was told at roll call that the captain wanted to see me. The chain of command for patrol officials is:

> Squad *Sergeant* (me)
> Platoon *Lieutenant* (Lieutenant Lewis)
> Section *Captain*
> District *Inspector*
> *Deputy Chief* (Commander of Patrol Division, Field Operations Bureau)
> *Assistant* Chief (Head of Field Operations Bureau)
> *Chief of Police* (Jerry V. Wilson)

At three o'clock, I reported to Captain Stolz. The men pronounced his name as Stowles, which is how I had thought he spelled it until I saw it written some years earlier. I had met him when I was in Personnel, because he then worked as a supervisor in the Property Division and I had had to hire secretaries for him. At the time, he had struck me as being somewhat fatherly and quite pleasant. He was short, plump, yet stood very erect. I had particularly liked his clipped, efficient way of speaking. He had a trace of an accent, and someone in Personnel told me he had been born in Switzerland, spent time in England and then had come to this country.

Captain Stolz greeted me graciously and invited me to sit down. He asked how I was getting along, and I told him I felt I was learning a lot but knew I still needed much more street experience. I was beginning to feel at ease with him and I appreciated his interest.

"I gather you're in favor of putting women on patrol."

"Yes, sir."

"And you feel women are capable of performing the same duties as men."

"Yes, sir. Not all women. But not all men make good police officers either. I think it's a selective job and a qualified woman can handle it."

"As effectively as an equally qualified man?" Captain Stolz persisted.

"Yes, sir. Of course it will take some time before we can really evaluate the program properly. But I understand some of the new women who've had street experience are doing good work."

Captain Stolz sat erect in his chair. "I have just come back from a sergeants' conference. It was—uh—male sergeants who were attending." I waited. "A number of the sergeants were quite upset about having to supervise female patrol officers." Still I waited to see what he was getting at. "They were saying there are times—" Captain Stolz hesitated. When he continued, his words were more clipped. "There are times when they don't know how to handle the women." He watched me for my reaction.

"I'm sorry, sir, but I don't know what you mean."

The captain looked embarrassed and annoyed. "I mean women have problems—that is, the sergeants were saying the women had problems at certain times of the month and they don't know quite how to handle these women."

Light dawned. "Oh for crying out loud—sir. I think your sergeants are really being gullible. If a woman is tricky, she might try some excuse like that, but it's certainly not legitimate if she wants to be a *police* officer."

Stolz looked startled. "What's not legitimate?"

"Calling in sick once a month is not legitimate and it's the sergeants' fault if they put up with it."

"But women—" Stolz seemed totally flustered. "You know, I don't even discuss this with my wife!"

"Sir, there are going to be some women who can handle patrol and some who can't. If an individual woman can't do a particular thing, then I think she has to be treated just like a man who can't do a particular thing. A woman who has to stay out from work every time she gets her period probably shouldn't even have a desk job, much less be asking for patrol."

"I didn't realize it was an individual matter," Stolz mumbled. Abruptly he changed the subject. "The sergeants were also concerned about the safety of the women they send out."

"And the men, I assume."

He gave me a long look.

I thought I'd better ease up. "You know, Chief Wilson

said recently that in a sense he wasn't worried about women getting hurt. If they're doing their jobs, eventually it's bound to happen. He said no doubt the bigger problem would be the first time a man who's the partner of a policewoman gets hurt or shot, and I agree with him. There's going to be a lot of second-guessing about whether that policeman would have been safer with a male partner—whether the woman backed him up well enough. I think every woman will have to prove herself individually on this ground."

"You have a pretty hard-nosed attitude about all of this, Abrecht."

"I don't see how else women can expect to be treated equally, sir."

Stolz eyed me coldly. "Have you run into any problems on the street, yet?"

"No, sir. So far it's been fairly quiet."

Stolz stood up. "Well, Sergeant, you've only been here a few days. That still leaves you a year of probation to find out how you handle yourself."

"Yes, sir," I said.

"I wish we could all share your confidence." Stolz dismissed me.

My hands were cold and moist from tension as I left his office. I wondered what he would think if he knew all the personal doubts I really had.

I spent a good part of Thursday and Friday, my days off, worrying—to myself, and to Gary when he was around. Was I doing my job? Would I soon learn what my job was? I reviewed the meanings of the different radio codes and went around translating clock hours into military time and vice-versa. I certainly couldn't concentrate on my law studies. I told Gary it seemed incredible that sergeants weren't given experienced partners for several weeks to break them in. Gary pointed out that most sergeants came to the job with at least three years' street experience as patrol officers. That didn't help me at all.

10

DISCRETION

The work of a patrol sergeant is highly discretionary. While all runs are assigned to specific scout units, the sergeant generally decides for himself which calls to respond to. Since there are about seven times as many officers as officials on the streets, the sergeant limits his response to those scenes where he is apt to be needed. The rest he learns about when he checks an officer's report.

Certain serious calls automatically require the presence of an official. But which sergeant will respond depends on who is available, close by and first to volunteer on the radio. In matters of discipline or signing reports a sergeant usually works with the officers in his own squad. But on the street, especially in an emergency situation, all sergeants are responsible for all officers in their district.

When something happens on a quiet tour, everyone tries to be the first to volunteer. Extra sergeants ride in to see what is happening or whether they can be of help. But unless more than one official is needed, they generally stay in the background close to their radios. The first official on the scene takes command.

One day during my second week of work, I responded to the scene of a holdup. When I arrived, a woman was down on the ground surrounded by four male officers. A fairly large crowd had gathered to watch, some of them still in shirtsleeves in the unusually warm, breezeless October twilight. I spoke to one of the officers briefly and learned that the woman had just pulled a knife on the owner of a liquor store and the policemen were about to pick her up and put her in a patrol wagon. She wouldn't get up of her own accord.

I thought to myself, with a crowd gathered and a woman on the ground, it's better if *I* get her up than if a bunch of men grab her. If I handle it, the bystanders will have less reason to conjure up the image of mean policemen dragging some woman off to jail. Particularly if men have to wrestle with a struggling female, they have to grab her wherever they can, and if one of them happens to touch her in the wrong place, some citizen usually yells that the police are molesting her.

This woman seemed passive and sullen. She was already handcuffed and had been searched. I stepped in front of the men to ask her one more time to get up, and suddenly she became violent, kicking at me, trying to lunge forward as though she wanted to bite me while the whole time she hurled a stream of invective. "Get her away from me, I don't want no mother-fuckin' cunt near me."

I jumped back and one of the men moved in. The woman immediately became as calm as could be. She got up and allowed the officer to propel her by the elbow to the wagon. So much for my estimate of how best to cool that situation.

Another Three D sergeant named Lacy had arrived on the scene and watched the end of it. "You didn't have to get involved," he said.

"I guess not. She sure didn't like me."

I got back in my car feeling somewhat shaken. I wasn't used to this kind of abuse. In Youth Division we rarely had taken action with adult citizens. When we did, it was usually to accuse them of having done something bad to their kids, and rather than being abusive, they generally tried to prove to us how sweet and lovable they were. If juveniles under arrest were occasionally shooting off their mouths, it was to everybody in sight. But this cursing, directed at me personally, when I felt I had done nothing to provoke it, was a startling and painful experience. Then, to see a male walk up and calmly accomplish what I had tried to do without getting any flak really hurt.

Gary had told me you develop a thick skin. People who like what you're doing think you're wonderful. People who don't hurl a string of epithets. So in the performance of your duty, you try to operate in a clinical manner and maintain the philosophical attitude that people are not after you personally when they vent their anger. But obviously I still expected someone's attitude toward a police officer to correspond to the way that police officer treated the person. I hoped it didn't take long to get a little thick-skinned.

Although my experience riding with Lieutenant Lewis had proven that even an experienced official had some very quiet tours, I continually felt lost and out of the action. At first, this was true in one respect.

One of the calls that was apt to come out several times a night was for a man with a gun. In perhaps eight out of ten cases, there was no gun at all, and the ninth time, the gun was legitimate. But there was always that tenth time. So "man-with-a-gun" was always an expedite call, and was assigned to two scout cars.

A supervisor was supposed to go, although generally everything was over by the time he arrived, because he had to come a greater distance than the scout cars, which stayed within their own small beat. The first couple of times I heard a gun call come out for a location I might have reached, I didn't feel bad when other sergeants volunteered before me. Everybody expedited to this call. In view of my unfamiliarity with the area, the equipment and responding Code One, I hesitated to announce to the world that I was going in case I didn't make it in reasonable time. I went, but I just kind of slid in, inconspicuously. I was practicing.

The first time I officially acknowledged as the responding sergeant for a gun call, I sensed the feeling all police in this circumstance must have. It is, quite simply, fear.

You hear a couple of scouts get the run. You volunteer that you're responding, and immediately you think, "Someone can shoot me." Or, "Someone is shooting someone else." That's obviously the worst that can happen with a man with a gun, and it's what's on your mind. The adrenalin starts to flow. And it's a Code One run to start with, so you're flicking on your lights and speeding down the streets. That's a little scary all by itself, although it's probably more exciting than frightening. But it's part of the buildup.

Then you get there and you have to glance around and make a judgment because you don't want to jump out of the car if the man with the gun is poised at a window or behind a door about to take a shot at you. So you're tense, and you *are* afraid. But it's a perfectly normal fear and you ought to be feeling it. If you're not, you're probably not going to be cautious enough, and that's when you're likely to get shot at or cut. What each person has to find out for himself is whether he has a healthy fear or a stifling, paralyzing one. You quit the job if you have the latter.

Entering a scene, you're nervous in a two-fold way. First, you may be shot at, so you want to have your gun ready or at least be prepared to draw it fast. But second, you don't want to be trigger happy and do something foolish or stupid, like shoot at a moving object that turns out to be Mama bringing out the wash.

I had heard that police in some quiet districts of D.C. always drew their weapons when answering gun calls. In Three D, this was not automatically done, because such calls were so frequent, the officers took them more casually.

When I got to the scene of my first gun call, a whole bunch of people were gathered on the stoop of an old row house. The two scout units were pulled up in front. I jumped out of the car and ran for the steps.

"Hey, it's a lady cop," called a high-pitched voice.

"What's happening?" yelled a man as I ran inside.

I slipped my gun into my hand, carrying it low and close to my thigh.

In the background I heard a police siren and a moment later, Sergeant Lacy was on my heels just in time to join me meeting three officers with flashlights coming down the stairs.

The first one looked startled at seeing me. "There's nothing up there, sir—I mean sergeant," he amended quickly as he got together the fact that there were stripes on my arm *and* I was a woman. I noticed he was snapping his holster closed. I reholstered my own gun.

"Did you get a good look around?" Lacy asked.

"Yeah. It's a small building. We had a false call on this block about a week ago."

We all trooped outside where the people on the stoop waited expectantly. The officers started asking some questions, trying to find out who had turned in the call. Nobody seemed to have any more information than we did.

One old man asked for about the tenth time, "Well, what was it? What was it?"

I said in a tight voice, "It was apparently nothing, sir."

"Nothing, huh? Well, that doesn't tell me much. I once got *arrested* for doing nothing."

Lieutenant Lewis said, "Abrecht, were you working this shift?"

It had become one of his standard comments, and I hated it because I never knew how to take it. If he was asking me seriously, perhaps I should tell him what I had been doing. But I didn't want to make a fool of myself.

One of the peculiarities about my job was that my lieutenant didn't really know where I had been all tour. He might have heard me on the radio, but if he hadn't followed me around, his only other check was to go through all the reports that were filed and see where my signature appeared as the approving sergeant or where my name was listed as one of the officials present at a scene.

One of my routine duties was making up roll call. This meant deciding assignments, or cars and special duties, for every officer who would be working the coming shift. The sergeants took turns doing this for the whole platoon, which comprised six squads, or about forty-five officers. It wasn't difficult, but time-consuming, and I would come in at least an hour before roll call, which started on the half-hour before the shift itself.

In D.C., Patrol Division worked two weeks on a given shift. Every other Sunday, tours rotated, going from evening (3 P.M.–11 P.M.) to day (7 A.M.–3 P.M.) to midnight (11 P.M.–7 A.M.). Checking off Saturday evening at eleven gave me less than eight hours in which to go home, shower, sleep, eat and be back at Three D for Sunday morning's roll call.

For obvious reasons, the switch from evening to day shift was called "short-change weekend." A similar time crunch occurred when we went from day to midnight shift.

Ironically, in Third District, Saturdays, which were the busiest times for police, were worked by the less experienced people, since the senior squads and officials had their choice of days off and always took the weekends.

The police manual said you got twenty minutes for lunch or dinner. If you were alone in a car, you could go out of service, which meant you called the dispatcher and said, "Cruiser two-four-six, ten-seven-E—" and you gave the address. "Ten-seven" was the code for out of service, and "E" literally stood for eat. Many times I did not leave the car to eat for fear of missing something on the radio.

A two-man car was not allowed to go out of service at all. It just pulled up to a carry-out food place, and one officer went in and brought back some chow. As likely as not, the men would just be starting to eat when they'd get a call for a robbery in progress. Perhaps because of eating conditions as well as the stresses of the job, a lot of policemen had ulcers.

Others, like Gary, were underweight. Although he worked alone, it was impossible to get a decent meal in twenty minutes. Before the yearly February weigh-in, Gary would have to start stuffing himself and drinking quarts of milk to "make weight." For someone like me, who put on weight easily, the job was a good way of keeping my calories down.

One of the problems in describing police work accurately is that the dramatic episodes stand out. Yet in actuality, they are days or even weeks apart. Most police work is routine.

Family disputes, accident scenes, dog bites, false burglar alarms, citizens who are locked out of their homes, lost, drunk, out of gas, bothered by a loud hi-fi or a boisterous party, afraid they saw a prowler or heard gunshots or saw someone with a weapon, people unable to find a child or change a tire —these situations make up the bulk of a police officer's work and of the reports a sergeant signs. If they eventually account for a smaller percentage of a sergeant's activities, it is because officials select and respond mainly to the more serious scenes.

I was cruising a little after noon on my second Saturday of day work when I heard two scouts get a Code One run for a criminal assault and stabbing. I grabbed the microphone and said I was responding. A "criminal assault" always meant a sex assault. A cutting and shooting were identified as such, and if the dispatcher didn't know the type of assault, he simply used the single word. This time he had said criminal assault *and* stabbing, and I wondered whether the victim had been both raped and cut or whether she had managed to stab her attacker. I hoped it was the latter.

The address was on a narrow, one-way street. One scout car was already parked in front of the building. The second car was cruising farther down the block, waiting for a tentative lookout. I had to double-park next to a citizen's car. As I jumped out and headed for the door, another cruiser turned in at the opposite end of the block, braked at the corner and stopped half on the sidewalk. I recognized Sergeant Lacy running toward me.

I dashed into the building with Lacy following. How come he had turned up again? But my dominant thought was getting in and finding out what had happened.

Officer Rangely in my squad came bounding down the stairs and paused long enough to say he was going to make sure the ambulance and Sex Squad were on the way. "Third floor, rear," he added. "There's a woman been raped and the man's been stabbed. He was her husband." Rangely ran out.

"You better go down and move your car so the ambulance can get through." Lacy continued upstairs without giving me a chance to answer.

Dammit, he was probably right. I tore downstairs. What Rangely had said didn't quite make sense. Under the law, a husband can't rape his wife. One of the things about the marriage contract is that even if intercourse is forced, it's not criminal.

I hopped into my cruiser to move it and—the battery was dead. And there I was, the ambulance about to come, a rape and stabbing upstairs and me blocking the street.

Rangely was still in his car, so I had him pull around and we did a quick jump. As I swung my cruiser around the corner, I heard the ambulance arrive. By the time I returned to the building, the detectives from Sex Squad had also come. The stretcher was already on its way out with a man on it wrapped to his neck in blankets. Lacy was following it.

"Sweet Jesus, some fucking mess," he said. "That guy's intestines were just hanging out." I wondered if the man on the stretcher could hear. "If you ever come across that, push 'em back in. You've got to keep them wet. Forget the sanitary shit. If your intestines dry out, they can't save them and they can't replace them. You die. We learned that in the army. This guy must have done military time somewhere 'cause he had a wet towel and even in his shape he was stuffing himself back in."

The ambulance pulled away, followed by one of the patrol officers.

"What happened?" I asked. "Did you get it sorted out?"

"Yeah. An attacker came up the fire escape and in the window with a butcher knife. He locked the husband in the closet of the bedroom and began to rape the wife at knife-point. Her old man broke out of the closet and the mother-fucker stabbed him. I don't think the poor bastard's going to make it."

"How is the woman?" I started up the stairs.

"Calm." Lacy leaned against the wall of the landing, detaining me. "She says she loves him, and he'll be all right. Most of the people in this building are members of an outfit called the Church of Scientology. The neighborhood thinks they're kind of nuts but likes them. They're decent and they help people 'cause they believe in a lot of love and stuff. And they sure have their heads together. Sex Squad just told the woman that her old man was being taken to George Washington 'cause it's the closest hospital. They said she could go there too, but if she wanted decent rape evidence without paying a fortune, she better go get examined at D.C. General. She said she wanted the evidence." Lacy glanced upward. "They're going over the scene now, picking up clothes and stuff they want to examine. You may as well go back in service."

"Okay." I got the lookout on the rapist. Then I hesitated. "Lacy, just out of curiosity, did you hear me when I called in that I was responding to this?"

Lacy looked at me with a little too much surprise. "Was that *you* I keyed out?"

"Sure, Lacy. See you around."

"An-ytime." He gave me a slow grin.

"Keyed out, my foot," I thought, walking to my cruiser.

If two people pushed the microphone button, or key, simultaneously, neither knew the other was transmitting. Sometimes the stronger voice got through, but usually the result was just a lot of static, with the dispatcher unable to pick up either message. The people were keying each other out. This was one reason you were supposed to wait for an acknowledgment before giving a communication. Occasionally people keyed each other out anyway, but I doubted that had happened this time. I felt pretty certain Lacy had taken command because he thought that I, as a woman, couldn't handle the situation. Maybe I was being oversensitive, but I doubted he would have acted the same way with a man.

A few days after the incident, the Police Department got a letter from the Church of Scientology. It was read at roll call. The Church commended the officers for having handled the situation so well and invited the members of Third District to come in anytime for coffee. They reported that the wounded man was expected to live.

It would be luck if any of us ever found out whether they caught the rapist. Sex Squad would follow up the case from here on. One reason most police movies and TV shows are about detectives is that the stories of ordinary patrol officers don't have endings.

11

WHO'S IN CHARGE

I cruised slowly, watching the early Sunday morning activities. Most of the night people were gone, although an occasional prostitute was still looking for last-minute business or just now returning home. Residents were coming out to their stoops to pick up the morning newspapers. A couple of boys were shadow-boxing on the steps. Most of the dogs in this neighborhood ran free, but I saw an elderly woman escorting what looked like her grandson walking a puppy on a leash. I passed a couple of church excursion buses, and an all-night laundromat was doing a pretty good business.

Midmorning, I arranged to meet Rangely to sign a report. It looked as though it was going to be a quiet tour. I was just getting underway when a man came running along Fourteenth Street. He yelled and flagged me down. The report could certainly wait. I stopped and lowered my window farther. The man ran around the front of my cruiser to the driver's side and began saying something about his automobile when I heard the dispatcher call for "any official."

I pushed the microphone button. "Cruiser two-four-six, by."

The dispatcher started giving me a message and the guy at the window kept talking. His car wasn't where he had left it Saturday night. . . . Abruptly I realized I was listening to the guy and hadn't heard what the dispatcher said. With less than two months on patrol, I was still too green to be able to do two things at once.

I got back on the microphone. "Cruiser two-four-six, repeat."

This time I concentrated on the dispatcher and ignored the man, who didn't understand that I was trying to listen and continued his story with great agitation. I heard the dispatcher say something about possible suicide and ambulance, but I didn't get the address. I picked up some numbers that included eighteen hundred or nineteen hundred, but not the street. Again I asked for a repeat. The man at my car was hollering by now—something about a crumpled fender—and shoving some kind of identification through the window. What kind of address was the dispatcher giving me? The name of the block was like nothing I had heard of.

I knew I was making an absolute ass of myself on the radio, but I had to ask the dispatcher to repeat *again*. And this time he was obviously annoyed and thinking, "Who's this dumb female?" Everybody else in the district must have been wondering the same thing, because there were all kinds of kissing noises and moans on the air. Finally, though, I made out that the address was somewhere in the 1900 block of New Hampshire Avenue and it was in the rear. "I'll get near there in a hurry," I thought, "and follow the scout car in."

I turned to the guy waving his identification in my face. "Sir, please take your arm out of my window." I didn't know what his problem was, but I had already committed myself to what sounded like an urgent call. "Stay here. We'll take care of it," I said, but then I *left*. I did get on the air and ask for a scout car to assist the man at this location. But this poor citizen didn't know what was happening, so he just saw the police abandon him right in the middle of his distress. It was terrible public relations. Even driving away I realized if I couldn't wait for the scout car to reach him, I should have said something more reassuring or explanatory.

I headed down to New Hampshire Avenue and saw the ambulance responding. Beautiful. I had somebody to follow. I waved him in ahead of me, figuring he knew where he was going, and I rolled into an alley behind him. There must have been a hundred people packed in it.

I was the first police vehicle on the scene. I jumped out and the people directed me and the ambulance drivers to a spot behind a tall apartment building. A slew of fire escapes, each with a small landing, zigzagged down to a concrete square about half a level below the actual alleyway. Lying on the concrete, with blood all over the place, was a distorted body. What shocked me was how broken and destroyed it looked. It was a man lying on his back. His head was turned to one side, showing an unmarked half of his face. But on the ground underneath was a pool of slimy stuff with traces of blood. Was this what smashed brains looked like? One of the man's legs was bent back under his body at an impossible angle, and there was blood beneath his torso.

The ambulance crew went down and quickly determined he was dead. When they made no move to put him on a stretcher, a woman in the crowd gave a loud scream. "He's dead." She wailed the word, and for the first time I felt a real reaction in my guts. "Oh my God—" she screamed.

A scout car arrived and two officers got out. I told them the situation and asked them to block off the scene. They took some rope from the trunk of their car, and we got the crowd back and roped off the entire yard. The crowd's initial dismay at the man being dead was turning into a more disorderly mood. Many of the people were drinking from bottles.

Once we had the area secure, my next concern was to call for the appropriate units. We still weren't sure what we had here. A couple of people pointed upward, and soon most of the crowd was staring up at fire escape landing where a detached railing swayed out over the alley. It was on about the sixth floor. Someone said that was where the dead man had lived. I spoke briefly with the building maintenance man who told me the dead man had arrived, drunk, in the wee hours of the morning. He had come down to basement maintenance saying he had locked himself out of his apartment and wanted to borrow a screwdriver to try to get in. The maintenance man theorized that he had gone up the fire escape, leaned over the railing to reach his bathroom window and try to open it with the screwdriver, and the railing had given way. So it sounded like an accidental death. But one thing we couldn't explain was the absence of the screwdriver. Were we wrong and had someone pushed the man? Or was the screwdriver under the body? It was a question we couldn't verify because we could not move the body. In any event, it wasn't a natural death. We not only needed Homicide, but Mobile Crime, which is our movable laboratory equipped to take pictures and gather evidence, to investigate.

I headed for my cruiser.

Now the last thing the dispatcher had heard from me was my third or fourth request for the address. Sounding as authoritative as I could, I got on the air and said, "Cruiser two-four-six, I'd like Homicide and Mobile Crime at—" And I gave the location.

"Cruiser two-four-six, is that an apparent natural?"

"Two-four-six, negative. It appears to be accidental at this time." Accidental deaths, I had been taught, were a much rarer occurrence than naturals. Not only did they have to be verified as such, but the government liked to keep statistics on their causes.

The dispatcher came back on the radio. "Cruiser two-four-six, Mobile Crime says to have Homicide notify them after they arrive."

I acknowledged curtly. What was Mobile Crime waiting for?

I rejoined the officers out with the restless crowd. As soon as I appeared, a huge sloppy woman who seemed to be drunk pushed her way over to me, sobbing that she wanted to go hug the body one more time. I explained why she couldn't, but she wasn't listening. She started coming under the rope and I took her arm and shoulder, attempting to comfort her at the same time I was restraining her.

"We told her already to stay back," shouted one of the male officers. "Do you want a hand?"

"Nah, she's okay."

A man came up next to the woman and tried to lead her away. But she wasn't giving up trying to get past me. She seemed to think I would be more compassionate or yielding than the policemen. She sobbed, half-drunk but obviously truly grieved, and occasionally she shouted, "I got to say good-bye. I got to kiss his poor face good-bye."

I felt a little sick. I had reacted much less to the body than to this woman's emotion. The man was dead. He wasn't a pretty sight, but I could accept it. This woman was alive and suffering, and her anguish reached me.

When Homicide arrived, the detective took one look and went to call Mobile Crime. A moment later, Sergeant Lacy pulled in, and I felt a surge of annoyance. Lacy was followed closely by one of our Three D lieutenants—Clark—from the other platoon, and Lieutenant Lewis. My annoyance vanished.

Apparently it was a slow day and every official in the district was showing up. One thing they neglected to tell you at sergeants' school when you were learning how to command a scene was that for anything really serious, you would quickly be outranked and relieved of control by higher officials. Soon more officers arrived for crowd control.

The alley was clogged with police vehicles by the time the Mobile Crime van pulled in. First the technicians from the van photographed everything exactly as it was, including a shot of the railing up above. One of them pointed out a shoe scuff-mark on the wall coming down. I guess we were all impatient for the final test of moving the body, to see if there was a knife in the back or what. I wasn't even sure why we were waiting until a couple of more men pushed their way through. They turned out to be morgue men in fatigues, from the D.C. Medical Examiner's office, where the cause of death would officially be determined. A whole circle of police surrounded them as they finally tilted the body over. There was no wound, but sure enough the screwdriver was underneath. So everything seemed to fit together to support the theory of the guy having fallen while trying to break into his own apartment.

The morgue men slid the body into a bag because it was so bloody and broken, and then carried it to their wagon on a stretcher.

I chatted for a moment with the Mobile Crime technician and he explained their delay in coming. The dispatcher had telephoned that "Some chick up at the scene of a natural wants Mobile Crime." In other words, the dispatcher, after having had every indication that I didn't know what I was doing, just assumed I was a total incompetent who wanted Mobile Crime for some eighty-four-year-old man who had died in his sleep. The Mobile Crime technician shrugged apologetically. "So what the hell, we said make sure Homicide wants us before we budge."

On my way back to my cruiser, a captain nodded to me. With some satisfaction I realized I had finally been on a major scene where I had had a chance to do something.

"Sergeant Abrecht, this is Mrs. Booker calling."

I said good evening to our two-day-a-week housekeeper whom we were fond of and dependent on. We had bought a house—mortgaged and in need of repair, but roomy and full of character. Mrs. Booker had her own key, marketed for us, cleaned and generally gave our lives a little order.

"I just wanted to remind you that I'm coming in early tomorrow so's you or Officer Abrecht won't hear a noise and come shoot me." Mrs. Booker laughed with the barest trace of nervousness. She seemed pleased to be working for a police couple but she did not quite take our jobs in stride. And I suppose working in a house where the owners both had guns and there might be a police uniform hanging on the back of the bathroom door was not a routine situation.

Our friends told us they would call and ask for Mrs. Abrecht and Mrs. Booker would inevitably reply, "*Sergeant* Abrecht is—" Followed by out, at work, or sleeping.

The third time on one Saturday night that I heard a run to the same address for a family dispute, I decided to ride in and see what was happening. Sergeants don't usually bother going to these scenes, which are common and handled by officers. But three in a row at the same place? The first two runs had gone to cars not in my squad. This one was for Scout 92. I radioed the dispatcher that I was responding.

Driving over, I reminded myself that nothing in patrol work is routine. Earlier in the year, an officer in Seventh District had been killed while he and his partner were investigating a fight between husband and wife. They had separated the couple. The man went to get some belongings from a bedroom and came back with a shotgun under the clothes he was carrying. He shot and killed one officer, whose partner then killed him. An error in judgment had been involved: the man should never have been allowed to go into the bedroom unaccompanied. But in the face of the tragedy, this mistake had been quietly recognized rather than played up.

I met my officers outside the street door of the building. Willis Darr was black. James Merritt was white. Darr was short and heavy. Merritt was tall and thin. Darr was the senior officer. He was talking to a black man about getting inside.

"He says his wife has been calling the police because she wants him out," Darr told me. "The house buzzer doesn't work, so the first two cars couldn't gain entry. This time he decided he better come down and meet us."

Darr and Merritt went upstairs with the husband trailing and me keeping an eye on him. Darr knocked on the door. A woman opened it. She started to say she was glad to see us but then she spotted her husband in back. "Don't let him in here. He ain't gettin' in here by me." She closed the door part way.

Darr said, "All *right*. He'll stay in the hall and we'll just talk to you." He stepped into the apartment. "Now what's the problem?"

Merritt was standing in the doorway. I was against the

wall opposite it, and the husband was waiting a little distance away. We caught phrases of what was being said. ". . . have had enough . . . no good for the past two years . . . find his easy living elsewhere." And Darr's voice, "Then you're common-law married."

The husband approached. "Married enough to take my money for eight years," he mumbled. He came to the doorway.

"Just a minute," Merritt said.

"Don't stand in my way," the man snapped. "This is my pad."

"All right, mister, we're not keeping you out."

"Don't call me 'mister.' My name is Royce, *officer*."

"That's Officer *Merritt,* and don't tell me how to talk."

Their voices were rising.

"Okay, officer, you just let me have a look at that badge of yours."

"That's Officer Merritt, sir, and my badge number is two-oh-seven-six."

"Okay, Officer Merritt Badge Number two-oh-seven-six, why don't you just go ahead and arrest me," the man shouted. He stepped forward belligerently.

"I'm *not* going to arrest you, and don't tell me how to do my job," Merritt yelled back, furious.

The argument was absolutely asinine and irrelevant to what we were here for. I couldn't figure out the cause of the petty ego-baiting, but since I was there anyway, I stepped forward and said to Royce, "Sir, can I talk to you in this other room?"

Merritt gave me a dirty look and joined Darr. Mr. Royce and I went into a small dining room. I watched him carefully, but his hands were clearly visible and he seemed to calm down and relax once we were alone.

"Mr. Royce, what is the problem?" I spoke quietly, and Mr. Royce answered in a reasonable tone.

"We've been having trouble for a while, and the woman wants me to clear out, but I ain't goin' nowhere without my share of things. I bought a whole lot of what's in here and I figure I'm entitled to some of it, so I guess one of you is going to have to arrest me."

"What do you mean?"

"You arrest me, I can go talk to the judge and get what's mine."

So that was why Mr. Royce had intentionally provoked my officer. And apparently Merritt's ego was weak enough so he got hung up in the verbal baiting instead of detaching himself and trying to figure out what was going on.

"Mr. Royce, you can talk to a judge without getting arrested," I said.

Royce looked blank.

"There's something called a Family Court where a judge will hold a hearing with you and your wife and determine how your common belongings should be divided." I gave him a slip of paper on which I wrote the address of Family Court. "Mr. Royce, if you could collect some clothing now, do you have some friends you could stay with tonight and tomorrow, until court opens on Mon—"

Royce was angrily shaking his head. "How come *I* got to go? She ain't never gonna let me back in. And my things are all right here," he shouted.

The woman yelled an obscenity from the other room.

Darr came to the arched doorway. "She says the apartment's in her name."

"You mean the lease paper?" Royce asked. "Yeah, she signs that, but I give her money regularly."

"Let's get him out," Merritt called.

"That's what I been saying," yelled the woman.

"No one gives a damn what—" Royce started for the living room, and I stepped in his path.

"Mr. Royce, if you go to Family Court, you'll have a *legal* claim to whatever the court decides is yours."

Royce backed off a little. "You're saying I'm gonna have the right to get what's mine, and if she don't give it over, the police will come back here and help me?"

Royce's whole body suddenly relaxed. "Shit, I can do better on a Saturday night than listen to her rap. You hear, woman?" he called. "Next time I come in here it's with the police on *my* side."

I went with Royce while he collected some clothing. His wife stood watching and heckling occasionally, but now Royce's thing was to play it cool. He ignored her comments.

He accompanied us downstairs, thanked us and departed. With some amusement I explained to Merritt why Royce had been trying to get himself arrested, but Merritt was still hot and hardly listened. "He would have been gone long ago if you hadn't been around," he muttered. "I'd have shoved him out on his ass so fast—"

We went to our cars and a moment later I heard Merritt give the disposition. "Scout ninety-two, on that family dispute, argument settled—finally." So he'd gotten in an extra little dig at me. I still felt I was right. What would have been accomplished by hustling the husband out, only to have him go back later and start the fight all over again for the benefit of some other officers?

A cold, bleak Wednesday in December, toward the end of a routine evening tour. "Scout ninety-one, Code One, shooting in the ten hundred block of Harvard, the corner in front of the Amoco gas station."

Ninety-one acknowledged and I grabbed the microphone to say I was responding. My immediate thought was a holdup at the gas station. I sped over, expediting with red light and siren. Ninety-one scout was there when I arrived. I jumped out and ran over to where Officers Sherman and Mattera were talking to an elderly man who appeared to be slightly intoxicated.

"What have you got?"

Sherman, an experienced officer, said, "This man says he's been shot."

I looked at the man, who was standing up with no visible sign of blood. "*Where?*"

"In the leg."

I looked at the man's legs. No sign of a wound. And his only problem standing seemed to be caused by liquor. I glanced at the gas station. It was lit and doing business as usual. A couple of young boys were watching us from near the pumps. "Sherman, why don't you and Mattera take him into the men's room and check him out."

I went over to the kids.

"Is he shot?" one of them asked.

"She don't know, she's a lady," the other said. "Lady cops work with kids. How come you out at night, lady?" He was fresh all right.

"Shut up, Jeffrey. She's still *po*lice, so shut up your jiving."

"Does either of you know what happened here?" I asked.

"He *said* he was shot," Jeffrey replied.

"He was limping," the other boy said. "We were waiting for my uncle. He works here. So this dude comes by limping and I say, 'Hey, man, what's the matter with you?' And he says, 'I was shot.' So I told my uncle and he said call nine-one-one."

My officers and the man came out of the restroom. Sherman said in disgust, "He was shot. Eight years ago!"

"What?"

"He's got an old wound in the calf of his leg that makes him limp. He's very proud of it. He showed it to us. Wanna see it?"

"Oh for Pete's sake." I told my men why the boys had called the police. As I was finishing, I heard and saw Sergeant Lacy's cruiser screech around mine and into the gas station area. He had probably thought it was a gas station holdup, too. "I'll go tell the dispatcher what we've got," I said. "It should make his night."

"No report on this, huh, Sergeant?" Sherman was grinning.

"Nah. I think the department crime statistics can do without this one."

In my car, I got the dispatcher. "Cruiser two-four-six, no shooting on Harvard. Subject has an eight-year-old gunshot wound."

There was definitely a pause before the dispatcher acknowledged.

I saw Lacy speak briefly to my men, then get into his car and drive off. I waited, surprised, as Sherman trotted toward me.

"Sergeant Lacy says take him to the hospital," Sherman stated.

"To the hospital! Did you tell Sergeant Lacy the guy was shot *eight years ago?*"

"He didn't really give me time. I said it was an old wound,

and then he asked the subject if he wanted to go to the hospital, and the old guy said sure."

Lacy had given a direct order and left the scene. I was really irritated. Where did he come off, giving an order when I was already present? But I didn't have the confidence to countermand the instruction of a more senior sergeant.

Sherman and Mattera put the man into their car and a minute later I heard them ask on the air for Sergeant Lacy's cruiser.

"Cruiser two-four-two, by," came Lacy's voice.

"Subject doesn't want to go to Freedmen's. Request we take him to Washington Hospital Center."

Now I was sure Lacy would say, "Disregard." Washington Hospital Center was much farther away and made the whole thing even more ridiculous.

Lacy said, "Proceed."

I couldn't believe it. Then I got furious. Lacy was tying up two of my officers to take a guy with a healed wound to a hospital clear across town. And I was sure he had ridden in over me because I was a woman. As Policewomen's Coordinator, I had heard from other women about male partners being overprotective or taking charge. I had to say something to Lacy.

When I reached the station at checkoff time, Lacy was nowhere in sight. He finally walked into the sergeants' room chatting with Lieutenant Lewis.

"Hey, Mary," Lacy greeted me with a wink.

"Hey, Lacy." I walked over to him. "Tell me, is there some special Three D policy I should know about that says you take a healed, eight-year-old gunshot wound to the hospital?"

Lacy didn't even have the grace to blush. "Tell Sherman next time to be more specific in his verbal reports. He didn't state clearly that it was a healed wound."

"He stated it clearly to *me*. We had things settled until you charged in."

Lieutenant Lewis looked at the two of us. "Isn't she pretty when she's angry?"

I could have slit his throat.

12

NEW YEAR

Gary and I decided to give a New Year's Eve party. Since the social life of a police couple has to be carefully planned, we sat down with a calendar. December 31 fell on a Sunday in 1972. Gary would be working the evening shift, so we invited people for 11:30 P.M., by which time he would be home. I was scheduled for day work and would have from 4 P.M. on to get things ready.

We agreed to include all of our friends, both police and nonpolice, with their spouses or dates. The list, we thought, represented an interesting cross-section of backgrounds and occupations. In every couple, at least one person knew either Gary or me and had spent enough time with us so that we weren't worried about running into the problems we always faced at cocktail parties among strangers. At such affairs the host, in trying to get a conversation going, would generally say, "Meet our neighborhood cops," or something similar that linked us to the group and our work.

Whoever we were being introduced to immediately had ten questions to ask, usually starting with, "Oh! Tell me just what you do!"

So we would tell them a little about whatever we were involved in at the moment, and that would lead to more questions. It wasn't that we didn't enjoy discussing our work. Some of our best evenings were spent in heated debates among police friends and people in related fields. Occasionally this kind of conversation would develop at a cocktail party, too, and we would find ourselves talking politics, law enforcement theory, or public medicine and the treatment of battered children.

But much more frequently, the questions were, "Aren't you afraid?" Or, to me in a half-whisper, "What does your *husband* think of your doing that? Isn't he worried about your safety?"

The questions were understandable. Yes, I was afraid. While responding to almost any incident, I think most police officers feel a certain level of fear, although it's sometimes indistinguishable from a kind of nervous anticipation. It certainly does not affect our actions. And most dangerous situations are over so quickly that there is no time for real fear to set in.

I seldom went into any detail over this question. People who had served actively in the military would understand that in a situation where others are not showing fear, there is a contagious sense of "This is our job. Let's do it." And for over three years, my husband had been doing the job. Furthermore, in police work there was an enormous feeling of backup support. Just by pushing the little red button on the radio microphone and saying, "Help," you'd have police coming from everywhere to assist you. All these feelings and realizations had been building in me gradually since my Youth Division days. In fact, if I had to choose the one time I had felt most afraid since joining the department, it would have been during my first day of on-the-job training when, ignorant and inexperienced, I walked up the stairs of that tenement with Pat Perkins.

If people asked me about Gary worrying over my safety, I would say obviously it did occur to him that I might get hurt on the job. But balancing that in a way was the fact that he seemed less concerned about me off duty than he used to be. He knew that when I waited at the bus stop at ten o'clock at night after law school, I could take care of myself.

Sometimes I picked up, in addition to a certain curiosity and admiration, a lot of resentment, especially from women who didn't have jobs outside the home. If one of them learned I was both police and going to law school, there would be a kind of intake of breath—"Aah, how do you ever manage the house? When has Gary eaten last!"

I usually tried to give honest but quick answers and then proceed to something about them that would get them off their defensive kick.

One woman at a recent affair had come up and said, "Ohh, you carry a *gun!?*"

"Yes, I do."

"Do you have it with you now?"

"Yes."

"Where?"

"In my pocketbook."

"Oh, can I see it?"

Now this was in a crowded room. I said, "No, I'd rather you didn't."

"Oh, I want to hold it. I want to see what it's like. Oh, please."

She was so persistent that I finally had to be very direct. "I'm sorry, but I refuse to take my weapon out at this party, and you certainly can't handle it."

Several other guests felt a little ill at ease with the idea that she might be about to grab my gun, so they quickly changed the subject. "Do policewomen wear makeup and jewelry on duty?"

I explained that it was a question of moderation and common sense. If you had pierced ears, for example, you didn't wear hoop earrings, in case someone grabbed one in a fight. You could get an ear torn.

A man came up to me at another party and said quite aggressively, "I guess you obviously don't have time for children."

"Time to make them or raise them?" I thought. But in a sense, his comment was legitimate. Gary and I hadn't really dealt with the question of having children because of the nature of our jobs. With both of us doing shift work, we would need a baby-sitter who was always available and so reliable and good that he or she was really a parent substitute. Some police found this in one of their own parents. But I didn't know whether I wanted to have a child—or should have one—when I could spend so little time with it.

Our New Year's Eve guests arrived promptly, but one of the first, a colleague of Gary's, hurried over to tell me that Gary would be more than an hour late. He had had to lock up a man with a gun fifteen minutes before checkoff and was stuck with the paperwork.

Another man Gary worked with said, "All I want to know is, with you a sergeant and Gary a mere officer, who's on top when you two are alone?"

"We take turns." Gary had told me this guy had been asking the question daily since I had been promoted.

"Hey, when are you going to start working for *us?*" asked one of the Assistant U.S. Attorneys. "I hear you're about to finish law school."

"No, I've still got another year. It's taking four years because I'm only going part-time."

Law school had been far in the back of my mind since fall, because my job was so new and demanding. I did a minimum of classwork and finally had to take a leave from the department in order to concentrate on preparing for exams. In fact, I had just reported back to work a couple of days before Christmas.

Still, the idea of eventually going to work for the U.S. Attorney was appealing. I had initially started thinking about the law the first time I had had a battered-child case and, with an Assistant Corporation Counsel, had taken the infant before the Juvenile Court for a protective custody hearing. At that time I was unacquainted with the whole legal system, from police on up. A woman lawyer—the first I had ever met —had been head of the whole Corporation Counsel's office. She had encouraged me to think about working in juvenile matters. But every time I went into another part of the system, I would think, "Hmm, that's an interesting job." Gradually I became most impressed by the U.S. Attorneys in Superior Court. They are roughly equivalent to the District Attorney in a nonfederal city, and handle all serious adult crimes, from child beating to murder.

Sometime after Gary got home, he and I realized our party wasn't working. People's backgrounds were too diverse, and their social styles were so different that awkward situations started cropping up. The men from both groups were still getting along pretty well, talking sports and a little politics. But the women were in trouble.

The vast majority of police wives didn't work. Perhaps when they were first married, they kept their jobs, but as soon as the husband began to earn enough, it became a status symbol for his wife not to have to work. Now these women had mainly their homes and kids to talk about. As a group they (and their husbands) were very conservative. Many of our nonpolice friends were liberal. Which still would have been all right, except that the ensuing arguments were un-

equal. It was theory (smoothly phrased) against practicality
(bluntly stated).

One of our friends worked as a counselor for the Equal
Employment Opportunity Commission. She started describing
her job to one of the police wives, who was not only a racist
but an unsophisticated one. So while the EEOC woman was
talking about investigating the subtle forms of discrimination
that had replaced closed lunch counters and the like, the
police wife was going through the ceiling. "I still don't see why
my first grader has to ride a superhighway to go to school with
a bunch of niggers, 'cause if he ever misses the bus, the only
way I can get him to the damn integrated school is by
private car and *I don't have one.*"

By the time the party broke up, there was little mingling
between groups. All the police wives were in the living room,
most of the police officers were in the hall talking shop, and
our neighbors—lawyers, students and friends from church—
were in the dining room. Fewer than a dozen people moved
from group to group, able to find a common ground with
everyone. Most of them were college graduates who, like
Gary and me, had chosen to go into police work.

On his way out, one of Gary's colleagues commented,
"Hey, Bones [his nickname for Gary], you should have
warned us there was gonna be a gang of liberals in the place."

Gary and I decided that if we gave a party the following
year, it would have to be all police or no police. We felt badly
things had turned out that way.

Captain Stolz inaugurated the New Year by calling me to
his office. "I am sorry to have to tell you this, Sergeant
Abrecht, but I think you should know." He looked serious

and concerned. "I believe the Inspector is very unhappy with your work."

I felt myself flush and my heart beat faster as I stared at him in consternation and some confusion. "I'm grateful you're telling me this, sir, but I'm not sure what you mean. I guess it would help me if I knew what the Inspector wants."

"I'm not certain. Perhaps it is as simple as that you just do not have the necessary street experience."

"Well, sir, I agree. I mean, I admit I lack street experience, and the men out there have more than I do. But can you tell me if that's affecting my work in some objective way? Am I doing the job differently from some of the male sergeants?"

Captain Stolz matched the fingertips of his right and left hands. "You realize you have to be tough with these men. I know you're not one of the guys in the sense that you don't go out drinking with them after work. But you're still too nice to them. They don't mind your knowing certain things because—" He paused. "Being a sergeant is not a popularity contest. The men know there are certain sergeants who will chew them out if they get out of line, but with you . . ."

I was thinking to myself, "How do I take this? If my officers are putting something over on me, it's a valid criticism. But if I can accomplish my work without yelling and screaming, I take it as a compliment." Unfortunately I wasn't getting enough feedback to know which of these things was happening.

I said to Captain Stolz, "Even if you don't know more about what the Inspector thinks, do you have any suggestions as to how I can do a better job?"

"Abrecht, every time you see one of your men messing up, get after him. If he's out of service too long for lunch, call him on it. If he's hanging around the station, order him back on the street. If a report comes in with a misspelled word, you don't correct it. You're not a teacher. Make him write it over and pretty soon he'll figure out he better not turn in sloppy reports to you. I'll tell you something else. I can learn a lot about a sergeant from the appearance of his squad. If you get after them on the little things like polishing their brass and leather, the big things will take care of themselves."

Captain Stolz's logic on that escaped me, but I remained quiet.

"You know Sergeant Lacy? You know how he's always on the air and takes command at situations? Whenever a scout car gets a serious call, you should be right behind saying that you're responding too. Even when you're not on the scene, you should be giving orders over the air. If we hear you on the radio, we know you're working." Captain Stolz sighed in disappointment. "If you had had time to train with a senior partner—if *I* had had you in my car, you would have worked your ass off." He looked to see how I was taking the language. It was nothing compared to what I heard when he wasn't around. "I could have taught you so much. You would have been locking people up every night and in court every day. You can't imagine what it was like. We would make twenty or thirty arrests on a weekend and no one ever gave us any trouble. Or if they did, we gave them something to remember us by, and the word got around. Do you know that when the wagon was full, I could just say to some punk, 'Okay, bud, you walk into the precinct and tell the desk sergeant to book you to Officer Stolz.' And the guy would damn well do just that."

The captain went on for minutes, telling me "war stories" about how he used to handle tough criminals. I said nothing. I felt worthless. I sensed my face getting red. A whole emotional state was building inside me as this man, so deadly serious and at the same time frustrating, continued to lecture.

"How many arrests have you actually made?"

It was a direct question and I had to answer. I explained that I could count on the fingers of one hand the number of arrests I had made because in Youth Division we normally processed people after the arrest had taken place, and I had never been an officer on patrol.

Captain Stolz nodded. "It's such a shame."

I could feel tears pricking in my eyes, and I was terrified he would notice. Tears from me at this point would really be the clincher. I fought for control.

"At least try to get on the radio more. Try to get in control of things. Get to more scenes."

I managed to say, "Yes, sir," and I was dismissed.

My eyes were wet and full but I didn't have anyplace to go to cry. I just had to make it through the rest of the night. I left the station, forcing my mind onto the coming duty. We were short of cars and I was assigned to ride with another sergeant, a new man just promoted and transferred from Fourth District. I got into the car where he was waiting for me and considered telling him of my interview. He would be objective. Perhaps he could give me some of the feedback I had been missing and maybe help me evaluate just how worthless I might be as a supervisor.

He started driving. I had about decided to talk to him when he suddenly said, "Hold it!" and pointed.

An unmarked detective car was pulled over at the opposite curb, driver's door open. A woman was running away from the car. The driver was on the radio, obviously asking for assistance, but on a different radio channel so we didn't hear him.

The sergeant swung our car around. By now, the plainclothes detective was out chasing the woman. He caught her at the corner, saw our car and motioned to me as I jumped out.

"She was chasing a man with a knife in her hand," the detective yelled as I ran up. "I think it's in her belt now." I reached for the woman's waist and pulled out a fairly large slicing knife. "Can you take her? I was on a shooting call when I saw them. I'm Grable from Homicide."

The sergeant I had been riding with ran up. "Transport is on the way."

"Go ahead," I said to the detective.

The woman started shifting sideways.

"Hold it," I said. "You'll have to come with us."

"What?"

"You're under arrest."

"What for?"

"For waving this knife around."

We were two police in uniform, and she didn't resist when I patted her down for additional weapons. Nor did she struggle when I handcuffed her, a routine precaution before transporting a prisoner. Her passiveness meant I could take the time to open the cuffs, close them around her wrists snugly and then double lock them so they wouldn't get tighter and hurt her. It was a different experience from practice sessions at training academy, where they stressed the techniques for cuffing a resisting subject.

Just then a man approached us from a little farther down the block. "She was chasing me." My partner and I tensed visibly. "Hey, it's cool, man." The guy stepped toward my partner, spread both hands palms down and said, "Listen, I better level with you before you find *my* knife." Moving slowly, he withdrew a small blade that was stuck in the back of his waist and handed it over.

The transport unit arrived and took the man. We took the woman in our cruiser.

Within ten minutes of my conversation with the captain,

I was back at the station with my partner, our two arrests and their weapons. I had a feeling of incredulity.

Captain Stolz came downstairs to the desk when we brought the man and woman in. He stood watching me closely as I read the woman her rights. Then she started mouthing off. "This is private between him and me and we don't need no mother-fucking police to settle it. . . ."

My tendency with people who give me a hard time verbally is to ignore them and keep on doing what I have to. I figure giving them attention only makes matters worse. But now I thought, "God, I can't let her sound off like this in the station. The captain will think I'm not being forceful enough." So for the next few minutes, I found myself alternately trying to question and shut this woman up while the whole time I was really wondering what Captain Stolz was thinking about how I was handling things and whether he would have had a better way. Finally he left, and we processed her and the man.

Two hours had passed before we finished the paperwork and were back on the street. I said to the other sergeant, "You won't believe the context in which that arrest was made!"

I told him the story, and he was astonished at the captain's comments. "I don't know you very well, but my impression is that the men call for you on the street and count on you like any of the other sergeants."

His remark gave me a temporary boost.

I left work that night as soon as they relieved me, but the minute I hit the car to drive home, I starting bawling and I cried most of the way to our house. I had just calmed down as I reached our place, but then, knowing I was going to walk in the door and get all kinds of sympathy from Gary, I started crying all over again.

Gary was home with a next-door neighbor who was also a cop. They were in the living room and Gary called, "Hello." But I didn't answer because my voice was so choked up. I just headed upstairs, wanting to avoid the neighbor.

After several "Mary Ellens?" and "Aren't you coming in to say hello?" he finally followed me and found me on the landing of the stairs crying my head off. Of course his first reaction was that I had been hurt or something absolutely terrible had happened. I finally collected myself and replayed the whole meeting with Captain Stolz. Gary shook his head in disbelief. He simply couldn't figure out why "that asshole" would have upset me so much.

I tried for several days to be absolutely perfect. Although I didn't really believe that giving orders over the radio from a distance was appropriate—unless you were on the scene and knew exactly what was happening you were apt to make a foolish mistake or give a ridiculous command—I was determined to get on the air for everything and get to every scene.

Then one midnight, a call went out for a shooting at the Twenty-Four-Hour Store, at Vermont and R. Another sergeant beat me to the mike, so I didn't have the responsibility of getting to the scene as fast as possible. But I went anyway, thinking of Captain Stolz; thinking I might be needed, or it might be interesting. I was not expediting, but I was moving quickly, because there was hardly any traffic on the streets.

As I drove south on Twelfth Street, a motorcycle with two men roared out of the intersection with V Street and made a wide turn in front of me so that I had to slam on my brakes. It skidded by on my right-hand side and then headed north on Twelfth, moving into the correct lane.

"You dumb idiots," I thought. "If I wasn't on my way to a

shooting, I'd pull you over and gave you a piece of my mind or a couple of tickets." But I headed on to the scene. It apparently was not a false shooting this time, since an initial vague lookout had already been flashed on the radio for two men running on foot toward R Street.

Ten minutes later as I was sitting in my car at the scene, where there was plenty of help on hand, information came out from a witness that the two suspects had picked up a motorcycle and ridden off. There were two men on the motorcycle I had seen. And they were speeding, heading in the opposite direction from the shooting. Obviously they were the two wanted men. And I had let them go right by me.

I just about died. And then I pulled my next boner. I grabbed the microphone and got on the air and gave information that the suspects had last been seen going north on Twelfth Street. It was stupid because it acknowledged to the whole world that I had let them get away, and it wasn't even particularly helpful. I had seen them so much earlier, they could be going in any direction by now.

Later at the scene, I mentioned what I had seen and done to one of the detectives. I suppose I was still hoping the information would somehow be helpful.

"I hope you don't tell—" The detective stopped and shook his head. "You just keep your mouth shut. Don't you tell anybody you did that," he said.

The next night at roll call, Lieutenant Lewis gave a lecture on police responding to a crime scene. "What you should be thinking about is not just getting to the heart of it, but watching what's coming away from it at a high rate of speed. Now I shouldn't have to be telling you this, but particularly on a midnight shift where there isn't much traffic, if any of you see someone speeding away from someplace where you know something serious has occurred, that's the person you stop. You keep your eyes on *everything* leaving the area. Just because you get a lookout for a couple of suspects on foot doesn't mean they're *on* foot. Most people leave crime scenes in cars. So you look in the cars, not just on the sidewalks. Stop worrying so much about getting to the crime scene. Someone else will take care of things there."

Needless to say I felt mortified. It was a reasonable guess that Lewis's lecture was directed mainly at me. Everything he said was the sort of information a patrol officer would know from experience or hear from his senior partner. I felt the low point in my career had been reached, and I wondered whether I would ever be able to do my job.

13

EXPERIENCE

As winter progressed, my street experience inevitably built up. Certain occurrences became familiar. I had been flagged down often as I cruised my patrol sector. The effect is always initially unsettling, because you have no idea what you're about to confront. You're slightly keyed up as you stop and wait while someone approaches your car's open window. And particularly at night in the tougher neighborhoods, you're watchful and alert because you are literally a sitting duck if this person is some kind of nut who wants to be a hero and kill a cop. Of course a great percentage of times, it is a perfectly respectable citizen asking for directions or some simple help—and probably mystified as to why the police are acting so standoffish.

Several times I had been stopped around Fourteenth Street by men, some of them bloody, who had been robbed and perhaps assaulted by prostitutes or male associates working with them. It was a common crime. I had heard stories about officers who had been called to "meet the complainant in the phone booth" in that area. When they arrived, they would find a man hiding inside because he didn't have his trousers, which had been stolen along with his wallet.

* * *

I was cruising late one March afternoon when I saw a puff of black smoke rising from the top of a five-story apartment building on a hill in front of me. From a distance, I couldn't tell whether the smoke was coming out of a chimney or whether the building was on fire.

As I drove into the block, the puff got bigger and just as I reached the building I could see flames licking out of a side window. I grasped the mike. So far, this still looked like it might be a trash fire in just one apartment. The building was old and only partially occupied. I suspected someone might already have phoned the Fire Department. That's what usually had happened by the time we saw something burning. In any case, I didn't want to get on the radio, "Emergency! Fire!" and have the dispatcher say, "Yes, Cruiser two-four-six, we're aware . . ."

I pushed the button on the mike and said really casually, "Cruiser two-four-six, do you already have a local responding for the fire in the fourteen hundred block of W Street, Northwest?"

"Negative, two-four-six. Do you need one?"

"That's affirmative," I responded coolly, while at the same time I was thinking, "Better go get any people out in case this turns into something dangerous."

As I pulled into a space a little way down the block, I heard Sherman on the radio asking to be held for the fire. In my rear-view mirror I saw Scout 91 stop in front of the building now enveloped in thick black smoke. Sherman and Mattera dashed in the front entrance. At that moment two fire engines came from either end of the block, hemming my cruiser in. So someone must have phoned the Fire Department at the same time I was reporting to the dispatcher.

I looked back and the entire apartment house was blazing, flames shooting from every window. It had happened within

seconds. I couldn't believe it. More fire engines rolled into
the street as I got on the mike and requested additional scout
units to block off the area. I heard the dispatcher give the run
to several cars. Cruiser 242, which was Sergeant Lacy, volunteered to handle traffic control. That was good because for
one thing, I was locked in the block by all the equipment.
Besides, Lacy had been a traffic motorman himself, and he
was great at organizing this kind of situation.

Still more engines edged into the block.

"Cruiser two-four-six," said the dispatcher, "be advised
that Cruiser two-oh-eight is responding."

I acknowledged. That would be either Captain Stolz or
Captain Brown.

"Cruiser two-four-six, be advised that Cruiser thirty has
been notified." Inspector Hogan, Night Supervisor for the
whole city, I thought.

And I was still trying to be as cool, calm and collected as
anything when I realized I was on the scene of the largest
fire in months. All kinds of high-ranking people were on their
way because they now had word from the Fire Department
about how serious this was.

"Cruiser two-four-six," said the dispatcher, "do you have
assistance there on the scene?"

"Two-four-six, affirmative."

"We have just received word by anonymous phone call
that the subject who set that fire is in the block now."

Arson! I hadn't known enough about how fires spread to
even suspect it.

The dispatcher gave me the subject's description—he was
a fifteen-year-old boy wearing a green coat—and when I looked
out of my window, sure enough there was the guy sitting on
the hood of a car enjoying a grandstand view.

I jumped out of my cruiser, but before I reached him,

two officers in the area had grabbed him. They heard the message on their walkie-talkies. The kid didn't resist while he was being handcuffed. I told the officers to take him to their car, which was beyond the fire area. Meanwhile I would call for detectives and transport. My cruiser was close by, and the officers couldn't broadcast to the downtown dispatcher from their portable radios.

I made my call and then sat for a minute. My car was there for the duration because it was surrounded by equipment. I heard the dispatcher talking to Captain Stolz, who had evidently stopped somewhere on the outskirts of the action. I was clearly relieved of my command with all the higher-ranking officials now present. I wondered what I could do that would be helpful.

Finally I headed on foot in the direction the two officers had taken the arson suspect. It was a cold March night, and there was less heat from the fire than I would have expected. Streams of water were being sent against the burning building. I picked my way over thick hoses lying in streets awash with water. Soot and flakes of junk were floating everywhere. I kept walking and passing more and more fire engines until I thought I would never get to the end of them. For a two-alarm fire, eight engine companies and four trucks respond. Each engine company consists of two pumpers. One pumper sits by the fire hydrant and jacks the pressure up and pumps the water to the next pumper, which puts it out. The "trucks" are the hook-and-ladder vehicles. So that was twenty pieces of equipment right there, plus a rescue squad and an ambulance and the Battalion Chief's car, cars of the police chaplain, police and fire surgeon and who knew who else. We had about a five-square-block area completely closed off for all that equipment.

When I finally found the officers with the arson suspect,

Sherman had shown up. He said the boy had been with him and Mattera, helping them knock on doors to get people out and telling them which apartments were occupied. It didn't prove anything one way or the other.

We all talked for a while, and I learned that to anyone who knew fires, the black smoke I had seen was characteristic of a gasoline-set blaze. Apparently someone had poured gasoline throughout the building in all the unoccupied apartments, which also accounted for the lightning spread of the flames.

The detectives arrived to take the boy back for questioning with a Youth Services officer. All the evidence, if you could call it that, was very circumstantial. The detectives didn't expect they would be able to charge him with arson. Nonetheless, the anonymous phone call meant we could at least now watch this kid. If there were more fires at which he kept appearing, we might have some circumstantial evidence that would hold up.

One of the amazing things to see at a big fire is how well organized the Fire Department is. They have to keep pouring water on the building for many hours, but no one fireman stays holding a hose for that time. Various engine companies relieve each other, and the company on relief moves to the back line where a vehicle operated by retired firemen serves coffee. The police of course are included in this ministration, and I stopped gratefully and drank a cup.

As I headed back to my cruiser, a fireman who also had come for coffee offered me his raincoat. I noticed a lot of people around me were wearing them. I had been getting sprayed from the hoses and thought that was why I was so wet and cold. Now I realized that at some point during the fire, it had started to rain.

I turned the fireman down with thanks, regretting that

I didn't have my own coat in my cruiser. When I had left for work, I had just glanced out the window. It would have been smarter to listen to a weather report.

I had gone a few more steps when a man in a black slicker said, "Good evening, Sergeant."

"Evening," I replied informally before it dawned on me that this was Chief of Police Jerry Wilson.

The fireman who had spoken to me said, "I offered her my raincoat, sir, but she turned me down."

Chief Wilson glanced toward me. "She'll learn."

14

RAPE

There was an officer in my squad named Truman S. Snow. The men, predictably, had nicknamed him T.S. Unfortunately T.S. stuttered, which was a considerable handicap for someone who had to use the radio a lot.

T.S. would get on the microphone to the dispatcher, "Ssscout a-a-eighty-s-s-seven, I have a-a-a—"

"Go ahead, Scout eighty-seven."

And T.S. would finally get it out. But probably because he had grown up in a black ghetto, T.S. had a very poor command of the language. He also had a tendency to be long-winded, which you're never supposed to be on air time. If you have a complicated message, you tell the dispatcher you'll call land line.

Lieutenant Lewis had been riding me pretty hard about T.S. He told me I should think in terms of shaping T.S. up or planning to recommend him for termination if he was too dense. I became very conscious of listening for T.S. on the radio, because if I hadn't heard his communication, I couldn't correct him. The more I listened, the more it seemed to me that while T.S.'s manner was a pain, his actions were usually pretty sound.

Then one midnight shift, I heard the dispatcher give T.S. a run for a burglar alarm. Now, 90 percent of burglar alarm calls are false, but nevertheless, they're treated seriously at the moment.

T.S. got on the air. "C-could you r-r-reassign that r-run and hold me out to i-i-interview a c-complainant."

Well, the phrase "interview a complainant" sounds like you're following up on an old report which has nothing urgent about it. The dispatcher, hearing that, said, "Eighty-seven, you're *what?*"

And T.S. repeated his request to be held at such-and-such a location to interview a complainant.

"What's the problem there?" asked the dispatcher.

"I d-don't kn-kn-know yet at this t-t-time."

I thought, "Something must be wrong that's keeping T.S. there," and I started for the location T.S. had named. I figured the dispatcher would get the clue, too, but he didn't. He said, "Scout eighty-seven, take your assignment."

And T.S. again said "N-n-negative. Will you re-reassign my r-run."

The dispatcher was furious. "Take your assignment, eighty-seven, and call two-seven hundred." Which meant, "Call us and we'll ream your ass over the phone."

I switched directions and followed T.S. to the burglar alarm call—which turned out to be false. Then I talked to him and found out that at his previous location, he had been flagged down by a frantic man in a white apron who wanted help stopping a brawl going on at that very moment in his saloon down the street.

"T.S.," I said in exasperation, "there are other things to say besides 'hold me to interview a complainant.' How about 'hold me to investigate the trouble' or 'possible assault in progress' or 'there's a man here screaming for help.' Anything that will suggest to the dispatcher the urgency of what you are doing."

T.S. mumbled that he understood what I meant and appreciated my help. Then *I* called two-seven hundred instead of T.S. and I chewed out the dispatcher, explaining what T.S. really had had.

"Well, I didn't get the message," the dispatcher said.

"Okay, it was a misunderstanding, but you must have realized it was an unknown situation, and I think when in doubt, you leave it to the discretion of the guy on the scene. If he's that insistent to be where he is, there's probably some good reason." After all, I thought, you can always discipline him later if he was talking to his girlfriend. Besides, it's pretty awful public relations to leave a man who's screaming for help.

A week later, T.S. fouled up in a situation involving a foreign official with diplomatic immunity, and I was fit to be tied. There are a lot of these people in Washington, and they have to be treated with kid gloves. T.S. gave me a long, complicated explanation of what had happened. He was really a nice guy, but the more he talked, the more impatient I got. I have a tendency to speak too quickly and even trip over my words, and T.S., with his plodding manner, was driving me crazy. I had to remind myself that my own tendency was also a fault, but I wondered whether the force could afford to have T.S. on it. Then, the very same night, T.S. became something of a hero.

Scout 87 got a call for a criminal assault, or rape, at Freedmen's Hospital, where the victim had been taken. Usually an official will respond to a call like that. I was in the middle of something else and didn't volunteer. I temporarily let it slip from my mind.

About an hour and a half later, the dispatcher asked for Scout 87 and there was no response. A couple of minutes later, the dispatcher said, "Scout eighty-seven requests an official and Sex Squad at Freedmen's Hospital." So T.S. must have heard the dispatcher on his footman's radio and called back land line. I told the dispatcher I was responding, and suddenly it dawned on me that T.S. had been at the hospital for an hour and a half and he was just now getting around to calling an official and Sex Squad. I was fuming.

I went tearing into the emergency room and said in an outraged whisper, "T.S., you've been here an hour and a half. What have you got and why on earth did you wait so long to *call* us? Aren't you in enough trouble tonight?"

And T.S., bless his heart, not only turned out to be right this time but his slowness ended up being an asset. He had a fourteen-year-old girl whose mother had brought her to the hospital. The mother had told T.S., "I think my daughter has been raped."

T.S. asked what made her think that.

"She stayed out late tonight and she won't tell me where she's been."

Well, at that point, just about any other police officer would say, "Look, lady, take away her allowance but don't call the police. Unless you have more evidence of rape than that, forget it." And the officer would have been back in service in two minutes saying, "No criminal assault, ten-eight."

But T.S. said to me, "There was s-s-something about the w-woman—why she r-r-reminded me of my m-m-mother, and I just figured she kn-kn-knew her k-kid so well that if she thought her d-daughter would be raped, I figure her g-girl is raped and I ought to get to the b-b-bottom of it and someone n-needs to get b-b-busted."

So T.S. had sat down and talked with the mother, and it confirmed his feeling that she knew her children. The fourteen-year-old girl was very shy. T.S. said he could feel she was a little afraid of men, and he sensed even more that she was afraid of white people. T.S. asked a white nurse to leave him alone with the mother and daughter, and then in his slow, steady way, he talked to the girl about all kinds of things to put her at ease. T.S. wouldn't scare anybody, anyway, and here he was making this special effort. Periodically he came back to where she had been earlier that night. The girl had already given her mother several stories, including that she went to church or was with the minister. Finally she told T.S. that in fact she had had intercourse with her preacher. She was terribly frightened. From what she said, she had consented—or at least he hadn't *forced* her but obviously he had taken advantage of a trust and talked her into it.

The mother told T.S. their preacher was forty-five or fifty—a store-front minister who did other kinds of work as well.

At this point, T.S. had called for an official and Sex Squad. He still had no evidence of criminal assault, because the doctors had been reluctant to do an examination. Up to then, the girl hadn't admitted anything, wasn't injured and the doctors weren't going to violate her by giving her this very personal kind of examination just because her mother thought she had been raped. They weren't going to play truant officer for Mother.

However, when T.S. told the detectives that this girl apparently had just had relations with her preacher, one of them immediately said, "Where? What's his name?"

T.S. gave the name, and the Sex Squad detective said, "Good. Let me talk to the girl."

He explained to us that Sex Squad had previously had complaints against this particular preacher, but they hadn't been able to prosecute because the situations were always borderline. He apparently was not the kind of man who dragged complete strangers into his car. There had to be some degree of willingness. Recently, he had given a lift to a woman waiting for a bus. She knew the preacher vaguely, was drunk and accepted his offer of a ride home. She ended up having intercourse with him and later wanted to make a complaint. But she and the preacher were both adults, and there was not the kind of force involved that could make a rape charge stick. Nevertheless, the detectives were keeping a file on him because he seemed to take advantage of weaker people.

This time he had made a real mistake. Whether the little girl had put up a fight was not crucial. She was underage, and it was a clear-cut case of statutory rape.

The girl didn't know exactly where her minister had driven her, but she said it was a motel on New York Avenue, and she thought she could point it out. The detectives wanted to go immediately and examine the scene in the hopes they could find some evidence. But in any event, they thought they finally had enough on the preacher to make an arrest when they found him.

By now our tour was over, but T.S., as the first officer on the scene, still had to write up the crime report. He was slow doing paperwork, and I imagined he'd be at it quite a while. Some other sergeant on the midnight shift would sign it. I left to check off, and T.S. left to do his report. Since the location of the crime was unknown, he would have to leave that blank for the time being, but he arranged with the detectives to phone him if the girl was in fact able to identify the motel.

The next afternoon when I got to work, T.S. was waiting for me with an astounding end to the story. It seemed that the Sex Squad detectives had driven the girl and her mother along New York Avenue until the girl spotted the right motel. The detectives then went in to see who had been registered earlier in the room the girl thought she had gone to. There was a name vaguely similar to the minister's on the registry, and the detectives decided to search the room. They got the manager and a passkey, assuming that the minister would be long gone but that there might be useful evidence inside. When they opened the door, there was the minister in bed—with another woman. The detectives arrested him on the spot and charged him with statutory rape. When they searched a briefcase he had with him, they found it contained a Bible and a gun.

Everything preceding the struggle was perfectly clear. But the scuffle itself was so unexpected and brief that only a general impression and highlights remained in my mind.

I had responded to a criminal assault, and the dispatcher notified me that an ambulance was also on the way. So he must have been told the victim was injured. At about 10 P.M. I pulled up behind two scout cars and climbed some filthy, reeking stairs in an old tenement building. I entered a dark living room, lit only by a street lamp shining through the window and an overhead bulb in the kitchen. Three officers and a man in his early thirties were standing around a couch gaping at a woman lying with an old bedspread thrown over her. She was large, fat, about fifty years old, and apparently naked under the spread.

There had obviously been a fight in the room. Women's clothes were scattered around and furniture had been knocked over. There was also evidence of some kind of party having taken place: paper cups and a bowl of potato chips were strewn across the floor near an overturned coffee table.

One of the policemen said they were still trying to find out what had happened. Before calling Sex Squad, we had to get some feeling for the background circumstances. Did the victim know her assailant? Was there force involved? Largely because there had been a party, we felt we had to determine whether this was, in fact, a "good" rape.

The woman was too drunk to speak except in grunts and mumbles. Looking at her more closely in the dark room, I realized she had a big gash on her mouth, and there was blood pouring down the side of her face. She opened her eyes and when she saw me said, "Lady." She tugged at the bedspread, trying to cover her shoulders more completely but nearly throwing off the spread instead.

I sat down next to her, readjusting the cover and trying to get her to forget about it and tell us what had happened. All I got were fragments. "I don't know why he did it. He hit me. He tore my clothes off."

Even coherent rape victims rarely are explicit about what happened during a sexual assault. That has to be gotten out of them with specific questions, usually asked by Sex Squad detectives. This woman was in no condition to talk. The young man, however, told us a little more. There had been a party going on in this apartment, which was his. After a while, everyone except the injured woman had gone to another apartment in the building. When the man returned home after about an hour, he had discovered the woman, hurt and naked on the couch. He had thrown his bedspread over her. He had no idea who had assaulted her.

One of the officers was making notes for his report. I told another to call Mobile Crime, since they would have to investigate the assault, and Sex Squad. Ideally, Sex Squad people want to come first to the scene of a rape, look at the physical evidence and ask a few questions. They then drive the woman to the hospital for examination and further investigation. But when there is an injury, getting medical treatment for the patient obviously takes precedence.

The ambulance crew—two firemen—arrived and helped stand the woman up. I held the bedspread around her, wanting to tie it at her shoulder, sarong fashion. But she kept tugging it the wrong way. Finally I made the knot with help from the firemen, who distracted her. They're good about this sort of thing because they constantly run into people in all kinds of conditions. They managed to joke with this poor, fat, drunk woman and tell her she looked great. She finally started downstairs with support on either side.

The four flights took a long time to maneuver. Then, at the bottom, when the woman saw there was a large crowd gathered in front of the building, she utterly refused to go out. I couldn't blame her. The firemen brought a stretcher, laid her on it with a nice covering, and it was a better arrangement all around. Especially because she was barefoot and would probably have cut her feet on broken glass and debris.

One of the officers radioed the dispatcher to have Sex Squad respond directly to D.C. General. He followed the ambulance in his car, to take the report. I called for relief units, because by now it was 11 P.M., and those of us still on the scene were early platoon and due to check off.

Leaving a second officer to keep an eye on the crowd and watch for Mobile Crime, I went back upstairs because I didn't think the third officer should be in charge alone. The man who owned the apartment was eager to get things cleaned up, and we had to preserve the scene intact.

Within minutes, Mobile Crime arrived, together with a sergeant from late platoon, who relieved me. I left.

Downstairs I saw that the crowd had gotten bigger and more disorderly. There was one woman—a huge female—hollering and yelling at a large man about twenty feet from her. Several young girls were holding the woman back, while a few men had hold of the guy, who was screaming answers.

Just then, the additional scout car I had called for arrived. Two officers headed through the crowd for the building I was leaving. At that instant, the two sets of friends let go of the pair they had been restraining, and this huge woman and man started for each other with me and the officers in the middle. I stepped in front of the woman and moved her back, getting a lot of assistance from the people who had originally been restraining her. "Come on, mother, go in the house, go on back inside." They finally succeeded in pulling her out of the way.

I turned around just in time to see the man she had been hollering at break free of the two officers and turn on one of them, pinning him against the scout car. The second officer grabbed the man from behind to pull him off. Suddenly some bystanders jumped on the back of this second policeman, and the melee was on. There were shouts of "He didn't do nothing. What do you want to bust him for?"

I dove in, pulling off whomever I could get hold of. I remember one man I was yanking and had dragged back about three feet. He turned to swing at whomever had hold of him, and when he realized I was a woman, he just stared and yelled "Whaatt??" But it distracted him so badly he forgot about going back into the fight. I collared another man from behind, twisted hard and got him off balance and to one side. I'm not sure what happened to him. Suddenly a detective was at my side, helping peel people off. I dashed out and called for transport, and when I returned, the officers had their man cuffed and under arrest for disorderly. The brawl was over.

Our immediate concern was to determine whether these two people were involved in the rape. When we questioned them and the bystanders, it appeared their argument was unrelated.

The officers turned to thank me for my help. One of them bent and picked up something from the ground in front of their car. It was my plastic name tag, which had been torn off at some point during the struggle. The officer looked it over and handed it to me with a grin as sort of proof that I had been in there with them.

I was glad to have been in the struggle. Many men still felt that a woman was likely to freeze and do nothing. And I hadn't been hurt. But as I got into my car, I noticed I was trembling. It seemed to be from the abrupt physical exertion and tension. Yet I wondered whether I was also experiencing a kind of after-the-fact fear. Suppose some people had pulled knives, or more of the crowd had piled in? Suppose I *had* frozen and done nothing? For whatever reason, my hands shook most of the way back to the station.

I awoke the next morning with sore shoulder muscles. It took me a moment to realize the cause. While showering I found a bruise on my leg where it must have been banged into the car. Yet really the physical aftereffects of the scuffle were insignificant. In fact, the possibility of my being injured on the job had never worried me as much as it seemed to concern many of my nonpolice friends. My biggest fear from the moment I became a patrol sergeant was not so much that I would get hurt, but that I would do something stupid and make a fool of myself.

*   *   *

Whether it was connected with the warm spring weather or simply coincidence, we were getting a lot of rape calls. There was growing concern in Washington, as in other cities, about how rape victims were treated.

Occasionally I was present when an officer questioned a woman with a seeming callousness or cynicism that was inexcusable. Yet most of the men hadn't begun that way. Police got that attitude because there were significant numbers of phony rape complaints. Once I cautioned an experienced team of men that they must treat each woman initially as though she was on the up and up. We learned subsequently that our convincing victim was a prostitute who hadn't been paid. In principle I knew my approach was right, but at the time I felt utterly absurd.

Sometimes I felt I had an advantage at a rape scene because I was a woman. But victims' reactions varied greatly. Some preferred talking to men. Above all, the manner in which questions were asked was important. A sneering query of "How long has it been since you've had a man?" was embarrassing and demeaning. You could pretty well destroy a woman with the implication that she invited the rapist. Yet the information sought was vital. A brief explanation that "In order for semen evidence found in a medical exam to mean anything, we have to know whether you have had intercourse in a consenting way with someone recently" made the inquiry appropriate.

For rape to be established, there had to be corroboration of intercourse by force or under duress. Corroboration meant either a witness *or* any number of other kinds of circumstantial evidence. The most common were clothes scattered around, signs of injuries from a struggle and semen in the woman's vagina. But thorough investigation could yield a tremendous amount of additional evidence.

As part of a good medical examination, for example, the woman's pubic hairs were combed, the "samples" put in an envelope and then sorted out by a trained lab technician. There is a tremendous variety between different persons' hairs. If the police got a likely suspect, they could take a sample of his pubic hairs and compare them. Hairs are not as good as fingerprints for identification, but they can be valuable evidence. Fingernail scrapings could reveal clothing fibers which might match a suspect's garment or skin particles which would corroborate a struggle and also be useful in making an identification. Any clothes the woman had on when she was raped were always seized and checked for fibers, stains and so forth. The very worst thing a rape victim could do, no matter how messy or despoiled she felt, was to take a thorough shower and wash her clothes before calling the police.

One of the appalling deficiencies in D.C. was the difficulty of getting a good medical examination. Many private doctors didn't want to get involved in situations that could lead to court appearances and a great deal of time lost from their own practices. Even some hospitals simply would not examine for evidence of rape. They would treat injuries but would not document or testify in court. D.C. General was about the only hospital in Washington that made even a reasonable attempt to examine a rape victim promptly, thoroughly and with good evidentiary notes. The hospital had a separate examination room where rape victims went directly, instead of sitting around the emergency room with several other patients. Since it was also a public hospital, the woman did not have to pay for the examination. But like most public hospitals, it was understaffed and impersonal. Furthermore, many of the doctors were foreigners getting their medical

training, and they didn't speak English very well. This made
communication more difficult during the examination, and
it was a handicap when the case came to trial.

Most pitiful and distressing was how often cases were
mishandled and dismissed in court for lack of evidence. One
notorious incident in the D.C. papers had involved a George
Washington University student who had been raped. Even
though the man confessed, he was acquitted. A technicality
about the confession made it inadmissable in court. Yet what
was even more appalling was that the medical evidence was
so poor, the case probably would have been thrown out
anyway. One of the accusations at the trial was that the
student didn't resist enough, and maybe even encouraged her
attacker. Now this girl had been badly bruised and knocked
around, but there was *nothing* on the medical chart to indicate that. The interns either did not know what to look for
or were too busy or lazy to document what they saw.

I think a comparison can be made between the investigation of rapes and murders. When someone is murdered—or
even if they just die without a doctor's care—the body goes
to our Medical Examiner's office, which is connected with
the morgue. There, they have medically trained people who
are also trained in evidence. It's a real art. When they examine a body to determine the cause of death, they notice every
little bruise and pimple. And they know what to document,
starting with the position the body was lying in to the tiniest
physical detail found during their examination.

But only when someone dies do the Medical Examiners
get involved. For rape victims who survive, there is no such
expertly trained group. I heard that a couple of years ago, a
woman who either was related to or worked for one of the
Medical Examiners was raped and these people were so out-

raged and concerned that *they* examined her. They applied their kind of thoroughness to this woman and got overwhelming evidence of her having been forcibly assaulted.

The idea has been proposed that the Medical Examiner's office should be expanded to handle sex crimes as well as deaths. I think that would be excellent. Because what happens now is, you have doctors who know nothing about evidence, or investigators who know nothing about medicine. You need someone who has both these skills.

One evening when I entered the roll-call room, Captain Stolz was sitting at the center of the large table in front of the room. I took a chair next to him. Lieutenant Lewis was on his far side.

"Attention to roll call," I said in a fairly strong voice. The men quieted.

Lieutenant Lewis said to the captain—not so loudly that the troops could hear, but I did—"God, she sounds good today."

The captain gave Lewis a strange look.

Lewis had been on a new tack lately, saying flirty, meaningless things. He always chose times when there were other people around and spoke not directly to me but to someone else so that I would hear. He would say, "She looks so good tonight I can't stand it." And others would chuckle nervously. I thought maybe it was his way of easing up on his former harassment and trying to establish some kind of informal way of relating to me.

I called the roll. On hearing his name, one officer acknowledged, "Yes, sir—ma'am." It had been a while since anyone had made the mistake.

Captain Stolz had come to roll call to comment about a

criminal assault that had happened on a tour other than ours. He told the men that an eighty-seven-year-old woman had been robbed *and* raped. The room became very still. Stolz continued in a lower voice, "While I've got you, I want to give you men a word of advice to pass on to your wives or mothers. If you put ads in the paper for renting an apartment or selling a piece of equipment like a television or washing machine, don't leave a woman in the house alone. We're getting a lot of calls about people who are answering such ads and then going on to do—mischief."

Shortly after that, I responded to a call that went out as a plain assault. The victim was a woman of seventy-five. Being elderly and living alone, she was in the habit of phoning a stepsister once a day just to let her know that everything was okay. On this particular day she didn't call. When the stepsister was unable to get a call through and a neighbor got no response at the front door, a few relatives got together to check on the woman. She lived in a fairly tough area, and the stepsister was afraid to go alone.

The party of relatives arrived late in the afternoon. No one answered their knocking. One of them broke a pane on the front door next to the lock, and they let themselves in. They found the woman in the hallway, half-unconscious and badly beaten. They called the police from the neighbor's home; the phone cord in the victim's house had been ripped from the wall.

Police officers had a chance to talk with the woman briefly before the ambulance took her. She said that about seven o'clock that morning someone had knocked on her door. When she opened it, a man forced his way in, beat her and kicked her and she blacked out as she saw him ransacking her house.

We called for local Three D detectives, and Crime Scene

Search officers, also known as print men. The scene was searched. Fingerprints were taken. Everything seemed under control, and I left the house to wait in my car out front. I wanted to stay in service in case I was needed elsewhere. Sometimes I could do this by carrying a footman's radio with me, but often there were not enough to go around, and officers walking a beat or riding a scooter had priority.

About half an hour later, one of the officers came out. When he saw I was still there, he said, "You'd better go inside. They're having trouble." His explanation was an example of how the various special units of the department occasionally got fouled up. It seemed that the detectives, in searching the basement, had found a chair with underwear strewn around it, a bloody rag, and some cut lengths of laundry line that looked as though they might have been used to tie someone up. The elderly woman had not mentioned a sexual assault, and because of her age, the police hadn't looked for it initially.

Now the detectives and the search officers were just local men. Having found this new evidence, they had decided this was turning into a bigger scene than they could handle without permission from the downtown unit that ran the Mobile Crime vehicles. Mobile Crime might want to send a van with its better-trained technicians and better cameras and evidence-gathering equipment. But when the local print men called, apparently Mobile Crime had neither given them permission to go ahead and process the scene nor said they would come themselves. The search officers were left hanging, and the man speaking to me said, "They're calling Captain Stolz right now."

I went dashing into the house. Captain Stolz had to be notified in any case because of the seriousness of the crime, but I hoped I could settle the disagreement between units first. But they already had the captain and were telling him the situation. I heard one officer say, "Yes, the sergeant just walked in." So I got on the phone with Captain Stolz and told him I had just been alerted to what was happening. He said he would phone Mobile Crime and get it straight.

The Mobile Crime man arrived shortly, slightly shaken and red-faced. Captain Stolz had chewed him out unmercifully. I had been through it myself and knew how he felt. I decided it was time we cleared things up, and as each group explained its side of the story, it turned out to have been a big misunderstanding. The Mobile Crime people had been left with the impression that the detectives were going to look over the scene once more, try to determine whether there had been a sexual assault, and call Mobile Crime back so they could decide jointly who should process the scene. The district search officers thought Mobile Crime was just undecided and unwilling to say who was to do what.

The Mobile Crime people were particularly upset at having the captain involved. I mentioned that he liked to be notified directly, not through the usual chain of command, of everything before it happened. I promised I would speak to him later and smooth things over.

Sex Squad was called and went directly to the hospital. Mobile Crime took over at the house, and I left shortly afterward.

The next day the story was in *The Washington Post* under the "Crime and Justice" column. The woman was identified, and Sibley Memorial Hospital reported her condition as fair. I wondered whether there had been a sexual assault. The newspaper hadn't mentioned it, but they might have picked up the story from an early teletype. The fact that they used her name indicated they had no inkling of a rape, since there was a general understanding with the press that juveniles or women who had been sexually assaulted were not named.

I had a busy week and, as often happens, never found out more about the case. But a couple of things stayed in my mind. First, there was the picture of the relatives trying to ascertain what if anything had been taken. They weren't close enough to the victim to tell whether jewelry, silver or other small objects were missing, and they were distressed by the whole procedure. In an effort to make small talk and cheer them up a little, several of us commented on how immaculately this seventy-five-year-old woman kept her place. And I remember one of the relatives replying, "Well, I guess for a woman of her age it's pretty good." Suggesting that the rest of this family were neater.

The other thing I had noticed made the possibility of a sexual assault all the more tragic. There had been little plastic Jesuses and crucifixes and pictures of the Infant and Madonna all over the house, particularly in the bedroom. You could see that this was a religious Catholic woman, the kind of person who, if she had been sexually assaulted in her basement, would probably have wished to die.

On the way to a rape call, it is impossible to predict the emotional state in which you will find the woman. I responded to two criminal assaults on successive tours where both victims were relatively young, middle-class white women.

The first one, a girl of twenty-two, had been hysterical and was still sobbing terribly when I arrived. The officers filled me in on the story, which they had gotten mostly from a man the girl had gone to for help.

She was home alone in a house where she and several other people rented individual rooms. A man came to the door in a T-shirt, faded blue work pants and a blue hardhat, like that of a construction worker. He said he was "looking for the meter" and he didn't see it outside. Was it inside and could he read it?

She said, "I just live here. Could you come back when the owner of the house is at home?"

"Oh, that's not necessary. It'll only take a minute. Is it in the basement?"

Mostly because the man seemed so sure of what he was doing, the girl said, "Yes, it is." And she directed him to the basement.

He went down and wandered around for a minute and then asked, "Where's the light switch?"

And from the top of the stairs the girl told him. But he said, "I can't find it. Will you show me?"

So she went down to the basement, where he grabbed her, raped her at knife-point and took off.

It was such a stereotyped situation: the man who thought up a plausible reason for gaining entry to the house; the girl alone who didn't ask for identification or try to phone his employer even though he didn't really look the part of someone whose job was to go around reading meters.

Afterward, the girl had fled from the house and down the street to a parking lot, where she found the owner, whom everybody on the block knew. He was black, in his late thirties, and a month before, he had helped organize a meeting about the growing danger of the neighborhood and the need for everyone to look out for each other. The girl blurted the story to him. He was the one who called the police. As a result, the cars assigned to the run were actually told, "Sexual assault just occurred in the parking lot at—" And that's where they responded.

The officers found the girl, got the story straight and then had her sit in the back of their car. They didn't want to let her reenter the house until Mobile Crime arrived. This caused a considerable delay. Although it had been a quiet morning in Three D, Mobile Crime was out on a bank holdup and a homicide.

When the van did arrive, the detectives let the girl sit in the living room and try to calm down. She never did, really. She managed to collect herself enough to call her boyfriend, but when he came, she broke down again. The officers in charge of the scene were extremely considerate. They stuck to the facts they needed for their report and left all the detailed questions to Sex Squad. There was no thought in anybody's mind that she was making up a story.

After another lengthy delay over the choice of a hospital, the girl was finally sent upstairs to take off all the clothes she had had on when she was raped, put them in a bag for the crime lab and dress in something else. Off to one side, the Sex Squad detective said to me, "I just hate these rape cases. They take so long and you get so emotionally involved. I'd like a good homicide once in a while. There, you've just got the body and you call the morgue."

Apart from the activity within the house, we were talking outside to neighborhood people who might have information. We heard that within half an hour of the assault, the parking lot owner had posted notices on practically every tree in the block offering a reward for anybody who found the assailant. Someone gave more details about the construction hat the rapist had been wearing. Someone else told the officers that they had seen the man and he had been in sneakers. This didn't strike me as strange at first, but a number of cars, upon getting the lookout, immediately started checking all the construction sites in the area. The assault had occurred at about noon, and they thought maybe the man had been a construction worker on his lunch break. One foreman, upon hearing the sneaker part, told an officer, "I don't *let* anyone on my construction site in sneakers. It's a hazard. Something could fall and cut off your toes."

So the guy was *not* a real construction worker, and the department redoubled its efforts at combing the neighborhood for a black man in a hardhat and sneakers—a combination now known to be rare.

I made a mental note to myself and also phoned my sister later that afternoon. She lived within a few blocks of the rape in a building with many female tenants and people coming and going all the time, so front-door security wasn't great.

I had a feeling this case would be closed soon, because the man's pattern was unusually intelligent and clear.

The following day I responded to a rape which also happened near noon. This time the young woman was absolutely cool and collected. It turned out she had been followed into the elevator of her building by a man already inside the lobby. He pushed the button for a higher floor but, without her noticing it, left the elevator behind her. When she reached her apartment and had the key in the lock, he put a gun in her back and said, "Don't say a word. Open the door."

When I arrived, I found the young woman sitting at a table giving this and additional information to the officers for their report. She was upset intellectually, but in complete control of herself. And it was a good thing she was a sturdy one.

The officers who got the run were beaten to the scene by four men from Casual Clothes Detail Unit. So the first people this girl saw when she opened the door after having been raped were four scruffy-looking individuals with no uniforms who claimed they were the police. They arrived about sixty seconds after she had phoned 911 because they had been on the block when the run had come out. I understood their good intent to get at least a speedy lookout, but I thought they had made an error in judgment. I felt that having the lookout delayed briefly would have been less harmful than having this kind of heavy army arrive at the victim's front door the instant she hung up the phone. As it turned out, she was shaken enough so that the initial description she gave was not very thorough. Even when she added some details later, we never got a clear lookout on this rapist, largely I think because the girl had been blindfolded a good part of the time. Otherwise she seemed calm enough so she might have been quite observant.

There are some great stories about identifications that rape victims have been able to make. A Justice Department employee who was a criminologist was raped in Washington a few years before. She and another woman and their husbands were all having dinner together. One of the women went to the back yard to put out some garbage and was met by a man with a knife. He forced her back into the house, tied the two men up and locked them in a room and made both women undress. While he raped the criminologist, the other woman ran out nude to get help.

The criminologist did not resist the rapist because he told her he would cut her up if she did. But she kept her eyes open throughout and studied him. Just started at the top of his head and worked down.

When the Sex Squad detectives arrived, the two husbands were practically berserk, but this criminologist, completely calm and collected, simply began giving the lookout: such and such hair, forehead, eyes. Beautiful detail on everything.

She mentioned there was something funny and distinctive about his earlobes, and as soon as the words were out of her mouth, one of the detectives knew whom she was describing. The man had previously been convicted of rape and just released recently. Now it was simply a question of finding him again and rearresting him.

Women occasionally asked me what I thought was the smartest behavior if they were ever sexually assaulted. Usually they meant, should they resist? Speaking as both a police official and a law student, I would tell them they had to make a split-second decision as to which was more important: prosecution of the rapist or safety for themselves. During a sexual assault, a woman is least likely to be hurt if she submits, perhaps even going so far as to flatter her attacker. A rapist who is not sadistic may just rape her and go.

On the other hand, the way the courts treat evidence, one of the best corroborations you can have is physical proof of a struggle. So as a law student, I would say that if the guy is not armed, put up the damnedest fight you can, and the more bruises you get, the better. Of course if he's got a gun or knife, forget your court case and save your life.

But regardless of whether you fight or not, keep your eyes open and your mind alert. Then try to give the police every minute item you have noticed.

There was a story I never confirmed that was told to me in rookie school. We were being taught how to interview a complainant, and the stress was on trying to get kinds of detail that the complainant might not think to mention. About that time, apparently there was a rapist around town who had a crooked penis. It slanted to one side. A lot of women had distinctly noticed that, yet they didn't think to specify it, or were squeamish about saying it. But finally it became known from a few of his victims.

Now obviously a penis that slants is not the kind of look-out you can give all your cars to be on the alert for, because you can't see it if the man is just walking down the street. But there was also a fairly good general description out on this rapist. One day the police arrested him on probable cause. They took him in and did a strip search. And they nailed him on his crooked penis.

15

SUMMER OF '73

"The long hot summer" had special significance for me since it was my first summer on patrol. A lot of people were waiting for me to break. I had heard all the police lore, and now I sat through reminders at roll call. There were increasing numbers of people on the streets, tempers would grow shorter as the days grew hotter, and it was especially important for police to keep their cool.

A Black Muslim sergeant I liked a lot made a point of explaining to some of the newer men, particularly a couple of white officers, about ghetto dialect and behavior. He was in fact a serious defender of black culture. At the time, his concern was that the police shouldn't be arresting people for disorderly conduct just because of the language they used.

"*Mother-fucker* is a common expression, you understand?" said Sergeant Owens. "It's no sign of disorderly conduct for someone to say *mother-fucker,* because it means all kinds of things. You get out on the streets awhile, you'll find *mother-fucker* is every other word. Someone yells at his friend, 'Hey, mother-fucker.' That's a greeting. That's not hostile. There have to be circumstances that make *mother-fucker* disorderly."

We had an Assistant Chief on the department who was sensitive to stupid things police did that upset the black com-

196 THE MAKING OF A WOMAN COP

munity needlessly. One of his angry objections recently had been to officers who made a habit of concentrating on Cadillacs for random traffic stops. A car may not have gone through a red light or made any violation, but if there was a black person driving a Cadillac, something must be wrong. And this Assistant Chief wanted the harassment to end.

Well, one morning, an officer in my district pulled over a Cadillac driven by a black man. The Assistant Chief, who was off duty and in his own car, happened to see it. He immediately stopped at the scene.

To his credit, the Assistant Chief didn't barge in on the officer. But the moment the officer had let the Caddy go, he went up to his scout car and said, "Do you recognize me?"

The officer thought he knew who it was but said, "No."

The Assistant Chief then identified himself, asked the officer why he had stopped that car, and without giving him a chance to reply, launched into a lecture about police harassing blacks in Cadillacs.

The officer didn't interrupt. He just let him go all through it and then he said, "Well, sir, I certainly didn't mean to harass him. I just recognized Larry Brown and I'm a Redskin fan and I asked him for his autograph!"

The Assistant Chief could only smile sheepishly.

When the officer got back to the station to check off, he showed the football player's autograph around and told the guys that Larry Brown had been delighted at being recognized and had offered to give more autographs for anyone else who wanted one.

Sergeant Owens, the Black Muslim, loved the story, commenting that it showed what an idiot the Assistant Chief had been in not waiting to get the facts before going off half-cocked.

The officer, in a kind of in-joke, then said to Owens, "I was gonna tell the Assistant Chief that I had to make lots of traffic stops because my sergeant gave me a *quota.*" Quotas were definite no-no's.

I chipped in, "You should have told him that your sergeant gave you a quota on *Cadillacs.*"

At which point Sergeant Owens roared, "Yeah, man, you *should* have told him that Sergeant *Owens* gave you a quota on *blacks* driving Cadillacs!"

Early in the summer, large, unruly crowds began to gather at all police scenes. One warm evening Scout 91 called with a kind of quiver in his voice for transport at Fourteenth and Chapin. My cruiser was not a transport unit. In fact, we had so many cars in the repair shop that I was driving an unmarked, borrowed FID (Field Inspections Division) cruiser. But Scout 91 was one of my cars, and the officer sounded as though he was having some trouble. I rode in to see what was happening.

About fifty people were milling around Chapin, near the Fourteenth Street intersection. Their attention was on two scout cars on the northwest corner of Fourteenth Street. The area was flooded with peach-colored light from sodium vapor street lamps. I could see two people under arrest being placed in a transport vehicle.

I swung slowly through the intersection and pulled up facing the two cars ahead, my driver's side at the curb. I wanted to find out what had happened. But just then the crowd, which seemed to have been calming down, spotted my uniform and realized my unmarked car was a police vehicle.

Suddenly there was a new burst of noise. A couple of dozen people turned toward me, shouting, "Hey, look what we got here," and "butch" and some other epithets.

I felt that I was creating a sensation and giving the mob an opportunity for a whole new set of curses plus an excuse to become unruly again. I thought, "If it's the police presence itself creating a scene, then the preferable option is to leave."

I was about to pull off when I heard a glassy cracking sound and felt something bump my shoulder. A cheer went up from the crowd. An empty Fleischmann's gin bottle had been thrown through my partly open window, chipping it slightly and glancing off my arm onto the floor.

I stared into the crowd, trying to figure out who had thrown the bottle because I wanted to take him in. The mob was still roughhousing among themselves, but they were no longer approaching and they didn't seem angry or threatening. In fact, I was angrier than they were. But I had no idea who had pitched the bottle.

I pulled my cruiser forward. Another small cheer went up from the crowd. I stopped parallel to Scout 91. "Did you see who threw that bottle at me?"

"What bottle?" my officer asked.

"Someone in that crowd—"

"Did you get hit?"

"It just bumped my shoulder. The window partly stopped it."

"You want a wagon, Sergeant?"

One of our options was to call in reinforcements and arrest the whole crowd for disorderly conduct. "No. It's not worth it. It looked like they were calming down before I arrived. What do you have?"

"There was a fight in Vinnie's Bar and someone set off some firecrackers."

The crowd seemed to be thinning. "Let's pull out and swing back in a few minutes to see if they've dispersed."

I pulled away with mixed feelings about the incident. I still wasn't used to crowds. In the small Massachusetts town where I had grown up, there were no apartment houses, side by side, teeming with so many inhabitants that they created a crowd simply by coming outdoors. In D.C. I had already begun to sense the difference between everybody outside in the summer taking advantage of the cooler night air—maybe fooling around using language I wasn't used to—and a crowd to be wary of. Yet my experience was limited. I hadn't been in Washington for the '68 riots after the death of Martin Luther King. I had no memories of dealing with really hostile groups. Even now, I thought tonight's mob on Chapin had been boisterous and disorderly but not threatening. In retrospect, the bottle throwing, too, seemed less an attack or deliberate attempt to injure me than an impulse. Maybe in fact I was naive about crowds, and there was more danger in them than I saw. I just didn't know.

Later that evening I called to meet Lieutenant Lewis. I wasn't sure whether the chip on my window was serious enough so that I had to report it to Field Inspections Division. I mentioned the bottle and showed him the window with some satisfaction, because it indicated that I had been in the middle of *some*thing, which he still questioned from time to time. He said the damage was so minor, I should call FID in the morning and not waste my time filling out forms until I was sure they wanted them. Then he looked at the window and looked at me. "Bottle didn't get you, did it?"

"It just hit my arm and then bounced onto the floor."

"Hmph. If you'd had your window open all the way, it wouldn't have gotten chipped."

*   *   *

I was working until midnight. At about 11 P.M. I headed for Georgia and Euclid, to get a report from two of my officers. When I was nearly there, I heard a high-pitched *scream* on the radio: *"Ten-Thirty-Three!"* Which is *officer in trouble!* And then nothing. No location, no call letters, no name. There was not even an indication of whether the call was Third or Second District—or just a wise kid fooling with the mike.

I pulled up behind my officers and for a minute we all just sat, waiting. Cars must have been poised all over both districts, but there wasn't a thing anyone could do. We didn't know where to go.

On the radio, the dispatcher started doing several intelligent things. First he asked whether any unit had heard more than he had—a location or a call number? Silence. Did anybody recognize the voice? Someone in Second District said it sounded like the Two D wagon. Immediately the Second District wagon got on the air saying it wasn't him. The dispatcher checked the other wagons, which were all okay. Next he tried to raise a couple of units on calls that might have been dangerous, and they were okay too. Then the dispatcher stopped. About the only additional thing he could have done was to call every single unit, which meant perhaps forty cars, and that would have tied up all the air time. So we just waited. One of my officers brought over his report and sat in my cruiser while I read and signed it.

Abruptly the dispatcher assigned a run to two scouts for a shooting at Thirteenth and T. Within a minute, the first scout was at the scene and radioing, "Citizen shot in the hand. The wound in minor."

"Is there a policeman involved?" the dispatcher asked immediately.

"That is negative, sir."

The officer leaving my car with his report said hopefully, "The ten-thirty-three sounded like a kid playing."

It had been a funny, high-pitched voice.

There was very little happening on the air, because no one was using the radio for routine stuff. Suddenly a call came out for two more scouts for a shooting at Ninth and Florida. The scouts acknowledged. Almost instantly a detective car or SOD (Special Operations Division) cruiser with call numbers not in the usual series broadcast, *"Emergency. We have a policeman injured here at Ninth and Florida."* And all hell broke loose.

We had just gotten a shooting at Ninth and Florida; now a police injury that was not identified as a shooting. I wasn't terribly far away and I spun around, flipping on my red lights and siren, and flew south on Ninth Street. An ambulance pulled in ahead of me, siren screaming, and I could see a fire engine, a scooter man, the detective unit which had reported the emergency and two scouts. Cars were pouring in from every direction. We had utter chaos over the radio because everyone was responding to something.

I jumped out of my cruiser at the scene on Ninth. The SOD man, who turned out to be a K-9 supervisor, was the only other official present. The supervisor and a cluster of people were surrounding a scout car. Sitting inside was Officer Reginald A. Ollie, Three D, his head swathed in bandages.

"What happened?" I asked a fireman standing next to me.

"A citizen pulled the firebox."

"What happened to *him?*"

"He was knifed behind the ear."

"Whaatt?"

"Yeah. He's some lucky hard-headed son of a bitch. The blade broke off when it hit the bone behind his ear or he wouldn't be with us right now."

The ambulance guys came over and helped Officer Ollie stand up. I shouldered my way through to try to get a word with him before he was taken away.

"I definitely shot someone," he said in a tone that suggested it was not the first time he had made the point. "He's got to be here somewhere. I know I hit him. It was point-blank range."

"Was it over at Thirteenth and T?" I was thinking of the hand wound.

"Nah, it was *here*." He didn't sound nearly as bad as he looked with his head all bandaged up and he was able to walk, although he had so many helping hands that he hardly had to.

More people were arriving. The cars just kept screaming in. There are twenty vehicles in the uniform section of a platoon, and there were more cars than that on the scene, all with red lights revolving because everyone jumps out too fast to bother turning them off. Many of the units also had their spotlights on. The priority was to get Ollie into the ambulance.

"I'll ride to the hospital with you," said an officer from Ollie's platoon, which was the early one. It was past eleven by now, and this officer along with several others must have been back at the station and then raced to the scene. Ollie's own sergeant took charge of Ollie's weapon and followed the ambulance to the hospital.

Some officers shouted that they were closing off the block to look for bullets and evidence. We still didn't know what had happened. I turned to look for the detective who had first reached Ollie and nearly bumped into Lieutenant Lewis coming up at a run. He had originally responded to the *shooting* call at Ninth and Florida, which I had forgotten about, assuming it had been confused with this knifing. *We* were actually on Ninth at that point. Lewis explained that the shooting victim was right around the corner on Florida.

Lewis said the first officers on that scene had found a guy leaning up against the building. When they asked him what had happened, he had said, "I don't know. I just heard a noise and then felt pain." He had been shot in the stomach.

We all looked at each other and then started talking to the firemen and people who had been first on the scene. The scooter officer contributed his information, and gradually things got sorted out. What had happened in sequence was, Officer Ollie was taking a report at the scene of a traffic accident. Then he stopped to write a ticket on a car that was double-parked in the block. It was the most routine kind of job, and he had had no reason to expect trouble. Except they warn you at training school always to be on guard, especially against someone coming up behind you.

Ollie was sitting in his car writing, with the driver's door partly open, when a guy came up from the rear. He grabbed Ollie and started to drag him from the car, at the same time stabbing at Ollie's head. Ollie snatched the mike but all he managed to get out was "Ten-thirty-three" before it was torn from his hands and he was cut. That's when he drew his revolver and shot the guy.

Apparently the guy made it around the corner with his wound, which was less serious than some stomach wounds. And when the police officers on the shooting call found him there, he wasn't telling anybody anything, especially not that he had attacked a policeman and gotten shot in return.

Meanwhile, a citizen had come upon Officer Ollie sprawled outside his car. Needing help but unable to find a phone, the citizen ran to the corner and pulled a firebox. A fire engine would at least be some sort of assistance. So the Fire Department responded, discovered there was no fire, but an injured officer. And while every car in the two districts was trying to figure out who had the 10-33, the firemen were applying first aid to Officer Ollie.

At this point the scooter man, who had been present while Ollie was making the traffic accident report, saw the fire engine at about the place he had left Officer Ollie, so he circled back to see what was up. At the same time, the K-9 detective cruised by, stopped and called the dispatcher.

There were so many police at the scene by now—anyone who could possibly justify going was there—that they were causing confusion rather than being of real help. Both the eleven o'clock platoon and mine were relieved. I was told to help with checkoff and alert the District Inspector that we had an injured officer. But when I got to the station, the Inspector had already been notified and was leaving for the scene. A couple of minutes later while I was in the sergeants' room, an official came running in. "You won't believe this, but the Inspector was so excited he just cracked up a cruiser on his way out!"

The sergeant explained that he had been outside when the Inspector jumped into his cruiser, went into reverse and heard a smash. "What happened?" he asked the sergeant.

"You just hit the brick wall."

"Oh," said the Inspector. "Bad?"

The officer said, "No," and the Inspector kept driving.

Later I heard about an exchange between the District Inspector and Officer Ollie. Now this was a black Police Inspector, and the man who had been shot was black. Officer Ollie was white. And one of the first things the Inspector said to Ollie was, "I thought we gave you *six* rounds." Officer Ollie had shot only once. "We'll have to send you back to the range for some practice at rapid firing," said the Inspector. And he meant it.

Officer Ollie was back on duty within a few days. It turned out that he had been cut by a razor, not a knife. The wound, which would probably have been fatal had it gone into the soft spot below or farther behind the ear, was superficial because the blade had hit the bone and broken off.

Since Ollie was not in my platoon, we were seldom on a scene together. The first time I really had a chance to talk to him was several months later while we were both waiting for the arrival of a Homicide detective. He told me then how they finally had closed the case.

Apparently the man who had stabbed him had been with a buddy. When Ollie shot the one man, the other ran, hailed a cab and jumped in. The cab driver, like his passenger, was black. The assailant's buddy told the driver to get out of the area. Then apparently proud of what he had been involved in, he said, "We just offed a honky pig." He gave the driver an address where he wanted to go and warned him not to put it on his taxi run sheet.

By the time they arrived, the passenger was having second thoughts about having confided in the driver. He showed the driver his gun and said, "If you tell anyone what you heard, I'll blow your head off." And he jumped out of the cab.

The driver was furious, not scared. He noted where he had taken the man and returned to where he had picked him up, to find out whether in fact a policeman had been killed. He found the whole area roped off and he gave a detective all the information he had. The police went to the address, turned up the suspect and arrested him. He talked, implicating his "buddy" as the one who had done the real damage.

* * *

I did two radio shows. One was a taping at our house for the Canadian Broadcasting System, and the other, a local Washington program. The interest in uniformed women on patrol was growing.

The woman who interviewed me for the Canadian show seemed disappointed that I had never fired my gun in the line of duty. I explained that most officers, in D.C. at least, spend a full career on the department without ever shooting their weapons except at the pistol range. Anytime a member of the force does fire his gun, it's a serious event. He is automatically put on administrative leave while the department investigates the incident and decides whether the officer will be criminally charged or given a medal.

The summer continued. I was on my day off getting breakfast in the kitchen when I heard a radio news bulletin that froze me to the spot. Officers Mark Sherman and Earl Mattera of Third District had been shot. Sherman and Mattera had been in my own squad until a couple of months earlier, when they got an advancement to a car in another platoon where they had weekends off. The broadcast reported the officers in satisfactory condition after having been wounded making a traffic stop at 4 A.M. that morning. Despite their injuries they had managed to return fire and had killed their assailant.

Sherman and Mattera were on sick leave recovering from their wounds for most of the summer.

One of my law school friends who heard what was going on in Three D asked if I didn't, in truth, feel a little heroic because of the job I had. I said no, but if I were Sherman or Mattera, I thought I would feel damn heroic. Particularly because, although wounded, they didn't completely lose control of themselves or the situation. Later I thought more about the question. What it came down to was *whom* I was comparing myself with. In the context of the police, so many had done things so much more heroic than anything I had come close to that I could never feel heroic. However, in a group of ordinary, nonpolice people, I sensed the contrast in our lives and I did feel bolder than the others.

The approximate end of summer coincided with the passing, on September 15, of my first year on patrol. It was a date I definitely noted. Although I proved a little something to myself every week I was on the street, finishing that first year was significant. For one thing, the department called it the probationary year. I had had one when I first joined the force, during which time I could have been fired without appeal. Then, after I was promoted to sergeant, I had another probationary year during which I could be demoted without appeal. Most people made it through, barring some especially bizarre incident, but for me, without street experience, there could easily have been a number of these.

Another reason the date was significant was that I had finished my first summer on patrol and it had not been nearly as bad for me personally as I had anticipated. Nonetheless the hot months ended on a note of tragedy that struck me to the core.

We had gotten word at roll call one midnight that Narcotics Division was going to stage a raid. They needed an official and four or five officers from Third District to go with them. The lieutenant gave me the assignment. I picked three men and a woman from my squad. Search warrants had been obtained on the basis of information from one of the under-cover detectives for two apartments in the same building. He had been invited to a "party" scheduled to take place in one or both of these apartments.

My officers and I joined up with the Narcotics people at police headquarters. I was the only one from Three D who was told our final destination. This was a precaution to make sure that anyone who had a buddy at the location we were heading for wasn't going to have a chance to warn him of the raid. Probably it was a good idea. After we were in the car and on our way, I gave the officers their assignments—who would cover the elevators and so forth—and a couple of them said they had been to parties in that building.

There was some general talk about the raid, and vague attention was given to the radio. Earlier, as we had been leaving the station, a couple of scout cars had gotten a run for a man-with-a-gun call. Since they were common and usually false, nobody had paid much attention. Now, as we were leaving the district to go on the raid, we heard an official's call letters and "send an ambulance to such and such an address. Policeman has been shot."

We all froze and turned up the radio. The name of the officer shot came out right away. It was Officer Rufus Jones, a man we had just left at roll call. More shocking than that—there had been some reminders by the lieutenant about midnight being a slow tour but we should never let down or allow any part of the job to seem routine, and Rufe had said, "*I'll* never get shot on this job. I'm too alert." He had actually said that while the troops were getting up to stand inspection. And here, within half an hour, he was shot.

On top of this irony, there followed a radio discussion that left us thoroughly baffled.

The dispatcher asked, "How serious is the injury?"

"It appears to be serious. Officer Jones is rolling on the ground. He has been shot in the stomach."

"Is it a closed case?" Meaning, had an arrest been made?

"Unknown at this time," came the response.

But a moment later an officer at the scene called for a transport, which meant there *was* somebody under arrest.

The dispatcher acknowledged the transport request and then asked, "Is it a closed case now?"

"Negative." There was an awkward pause. Then, "Transport is unrelated."

Well, if the person to be transported was not the one who had shot Officer Jones, the dispatcher wanted a lookout on the one who had done the shooting and he wanted it in a hurry so every available police officer could try to pick him up.

"There'll be no lookout at this time," came the statement from the scene.

Those of us in my car were just staring at each other in bewilderment. Finally, someone else got on the air and informed the dispatcher, "It *is* a closed case. It was an accidental shooting—" And then came the muffled words which I heard as "by a sergeant."

"Oh my God," said one man. We kind of checked with each other. Two of us had heard those words; the three in back had not. The dispatcher never acknowledged the report, and everything else must have been covered land line, because we heard nothing further from the scene.

We arrived shortly at the location of our narcotics raid, and our attention shifted to the situation at hand.

The apartment building was a large one, with a man downstairs at a switchboard. We sent two officers in to make sure he didn't alert anybody upstairs. Then we all plowed through the lobby and to the elevator. We had a battering ram with us for the apartment door. It was made of metal, its circumference about as large as a telephone pole, and it had handles on the side to hold onto during a charge.

We rode to the floor where the undercover man was supposed to meet the woman who had invited him and find out which apartment the party was in. We all stayed in the elevator, holding the door open, while he walked down the hall alone and knocked at the apartment. A female voice answered, and as soon as the door opened a crack, we all charged in. The female officer grabbed the woman and pulled her off to the side while we searched the place. We found a shotgun behind the drapes in the bedroom, a revolver in a kitchen cabinet, and little packets of heroin spread out on the bar where you would ordinarily serve your drink setups. We also found about half a dozen room keys to various hotels around Washington and the suburbs, plus a photograph album of nude pictures. The woman apparently supported her habit by prostitution. All the male officers took a close look at the album. I glanced at the woman, who was already high on something. She could have been quite pretty if she didn't look so emaciated.

When we tried to question her, all she would say, in a kind of dopey voice, was, "I don' know nothin'."

Leaving me and a couple of officers to guard this woman and detain anyone else who arrived, the Narcotics people took most of the force down two flights to check out the second apartment.

Shortly after they left there was a knock on the door.

"Come on in," we called.

A couple of men entered and it was, "Up against the wall!" They were quite shocked.

The telephone rang once and I answered it, slurring my voice and trying to sound stoned. A man gave me a message for Sal to meet him at the Diplomat, which was one of the hotels for which we had found a room key.

The rest of the raiding party returned, surprised to find the three of us now holding three prisoners. They were also embarrassed at the outcome of their raid. The second apartment number had been a phony. It was the home of some dignified elderly woman living alone, and they had gone through her door with the battering ram!

What had actually happened was one of the men knocked, and the woman said, "Just a minute." Well, when you're on a narcotics raid with a search warrant and someone says, "Just a minute," he or she might just as well say, "Break down my door." Because the police know that in "just a minute" someone can destroy everything he's got—flush it down the toilet, throw the works out the window. So the police hit the door with the battering ram and there was this horrified lady. In what seemed to be a very proper apartment.

At first the men weren't fazed. There are some proper-seeming grandmothers who are beautiful covers for actual ongoing narcotics rings. The men identified themselves, got identification from her and started checking out the apartment. But everything they found just made the situation worse. The place was immaculate. The only booze was a bottle of sherry. There was just everything "Sunday school" about this woman, including her membership in a church group. The only pictures she had around were of her grandson, who was away in the marine corps.

The men withdrew in great embarrassment, promising to send our police carpenter to repair the front door.

By the time my squad and I were on our way back to Three D, our only thought was to learn what had happened to Officer Rufus Jones. By then the facts were known.

Jones had been in one of the cars sent on the man-with-a-gun call we had heard as we left the station. A two-man scout car plus a sergeant had also responded. When they found the suspect, there was no gun on him, but in his room in plain sight they found a shotgun and three hand weapons. They grabbed everything. As they were about to start down the stairs, the sergeant noted what looked like a fat pen lying on the stair railing at the landing. He recognized it as a tear-gas pen-gun. It was metal, with a clip so you could wear it on your pocket. He picked it up and took it downstairs with him as further evidence.

The police, with the man under arrest, were gathered around one of the scout cars deciding their next move. The sergeant was still holding the tear-gas gun. Nobody knew exactly what happened next, except that he was fiddling with it or just looking at it, and it was cocked. Somehow he nudged the clip or release, and this gun went off and fired a *bullet* into Officer Jones's stomach at close range. No one had dreamed it, but the tear-gas gun had been converted to carry .22 caliber bullets, and that's what hit Jones. Few things could have been worse in the way of causing damage at close range. A high-powered bullet would probably have gone right through, making a clean hole. This small-caliber bullet from the pen-gun went in slowly and just circled around because it lacked the velocity to go straight through. And it was tearing up Jones's insides as he literally writhed on the ground howling and screaming in pain.

The poor sergeant who had been holding the weapon when it went off completely broke down. The second official to arrive at the scene thought the sergeant himself had been shot because he was just doubled over the car sobbing his heart out.

Jones was taken to the hospital in critical condition. Dozens of police went to donate blood.

One of the best officers in our platoon had arrived on the scene. The next day, while many people were still second-guessing, some of them blaming the sergeant and most of them ready to kill the man who had had all these weapons, this officer did a fine piece of follow-up work. He went to court and got a search warrant and then, with a raiding party, went through the entire premises and found a regular arsenal. The man manufactured, repaired and converted guns of all types, and they got enough evidence to have him locked up for numerous violations of the National Firearms Act.

Jones was operated on. For a while, he was wearing his insides in a bag outside his stomach. Then there was a second operation in which they put him together again, but there was no way of knowing whether he would ever get back to work.

The sergeant stayed away from work for a couple of days, but he couldn't stand it at home. I would see him wandering around the station, a terrible wreck, having to be there but not really able to face anybody. Although he was a well-respected and well-liked person, I think a couple of the men who had cocky attitudes that they could do no wrong did blame him. But most of them felt more the way I did, although perhaps not as strongly. I knew it could have been me in his shoes. I would not have recognized anything unusual about the "tear-gas" pen-gun, because I just didn't have that much familiarity with weapons. If anything, my ignorance might have saved me, since I might not have picked it up in the first place.

Once it was known that Jones would live and, to some degree, recover, the sergeant went on duty again. I suppose he felt that if he didn't get back into things fairly soon, he would never make it at all.

In the days immediately after the shooting, when he was just wandering around the station, he had appeared less concerned about showing his emotion in front of me than in front of some of the tougher men. A couple of times I approached him tentatively and he spoke to me, saying how terrible he felt. Afterward I regretted, and I continue to regret to this day, that I never came out and said to him in so many words, "I think I understand, and I *know* it could have been me."

16

SECOND YEAR ON PATROL

Gary had been promoted to sergeant during the summer, after having come out number one on the promotion list. His new assignment was in Fourth District, which is north of Third. The boundary between the two is Harvard Street, so our running joke was that once we met at Yale but now we were meeting at Harvard.

One midnight tour I spent hours in the station writing reports of a traffic accident in which an officer cracked up a scout car. Such accidents required completion of at least five different forms. Often the supervisor's job was a paperwork zoo.

I got back on the street at about five in the morning and was called to meet an officer with a report at Georgia and Euclid. Before I got there, this officer was given a run to "check the man down in the thirteen hundred block of Harvard."

So I advised, "Disregard on the other ten-twenty. I will meet you in the thirteen hundred block of Harvard."

As I headed up, an ambulance passed me, but I didn't pay much attention because there were several hospitals in the neighborhood. Then I heard the dispatcher give another scout car a call to back up an ambulance responding for a *cutting,* Thirteenth and Harvard.

At this point I was pulling into the block and I saw there was only one injured person. I advised the dispatcher that the man down and the cutting victim were one and the same. I jumped out of my car and ran to where the ambulance crew had just put this man on their stretcher. There was a large pool of blood on the ground where he had been lying. Another pool was already staining the stretcher around his upper leg.

Since the man had lost consciousness, I asked the ambulance crew, "What do you have here?" I should have known by then that ambulance crews are only interested in getting the person to the hospital, not in any aspect of police investigation. As a police official, when I asked what they had, I was hoping for an answer like, "It appears to be a gunshot wound"; or "It looks like a cutting"; or "Probably the guy was hit by a car and got his leg broken."

What the ambulance fireman said was, "What do you mean, what have we got here? We've got an awful lot of blood and his leg looks like a piece of steak, ma'am." And they carried him off, followed by one of the scout cars which had arrived on the scene.

So there I was with the pool of blood and no additional information. Because the body was in the middle of the road and so bloody, my first thought was that the man had been hit by a car which had just about erased his leg. The dispatcher had indicated a cutting, but cuttings were usually across the face or arms or chest. If you were fighting with someone, you didn't generally bend over and stab him in the leg. I hopped into my cruiser and notified Homicide to stand by, because I thought there was a good chance the victim wasn't going to live.

Meanwhile, the second scout car had arrived and the

officers were talking to a bystander who turned out to be the person who had called for the ambulance. When I went over, the officers said he claimed the wounded man *had* been cut. We were about to split up and search for a weapon when I heard a voice in the background saying, "Looks like a Third District case to me."

I turned around and there was Gary. I had been so caught up in the question of what had happened to our bloody victim, it hadn't occurred to me that the body was lying on the Fourth District side of Harvard Street and maybe we had nothing to do with it. This was the first thing Gary thought of, but he saw all these Third District officers, so he just said something that would make me notice him and bring the victim's location to my attention.

"Well, what do you know, we *are* in Fourth District," I said. "See you around."

"Now wait a minute."

Of course none of us was really going to leave, because we didn't know for sure that the victim had been cut in the same spot he was found. But now a contest started between the Third and Fourth districts, each trying to prove that the assault occurred on the other district's side of the street, because our main concern was to reduce crime in our own territory.

We traced a trail of blood back to a big puddle by a parked car. There was blood all over the outside of the car, too, so apparently the victim had paused, leaning against it for support. Next the trail went over the curb onto the sidewalk on the Fourth District side of Harvard, and I thought, "Aah, good." But in a moment I heard a call from Gary at the other end of the block. "It crosses back over, up here."

Sure enough, we found the beginning of the trail on the

Third District side in front of an old vacant house. We worked our way back to double-check the route the man had taken. The early part of the trail before the blood began to really flow was just a trickle. Then the signs became bloodier and more irregular. The victim had managed to stagger down the entire block, leaning against cars, until he couldn't walk anymore and eventually fell in the middle of the road. Perhaps he had been trying to flag someone down.

Gary, now satisfied that it was a Third District case, left the scene. We put in a call for the local Crime Scene Search officer and returned to the house with our flashlights to look for a weapon. Suddenly one of the officers' beams swept across a large broken bottle. We all put our lights on it. The edges were jagged, and it had blood all over it. We left it exactly where it lay until the search officer came to collect the physical evidence. He took photographs and dusted the bottle for fingerprints. Then he started working his way along the bloody trail, taking occasional pictures and measurements.

I was feeling a little impatient with my inability to make a reasonable guess about what had happened when we got a call from the officers who had gone to the hospital with the ambulance. The victim had recovered consciousness. He said that a man named Bossie had cut him because he was jealous, and the person he was jealous over, Jimmie, turned out to be the bystander who had informed us of the cutting. So it was three homosexuals in a lovers' triangle, and that explained why the cutting in the upper leg. Bossie had tried to castrate Jimmie's lover. The lookout was flashed. It figured that there wouldn't be too much trouble finding Bossie and closing the case. Personally I doubted there would ever be a vigorous prosecution. It was a lot more likely that they would all make up.

*   *   *

News and gossip spread quickly within the department. We frequently heard about off-duty events, since private conduct affected a policeman's professional life.

A group of officers stopped after work for a few beers. They were all white, in an Irish bar. A black man entered with a white woman, and the officers, who by now had had some drinks, began commenting. The black man replied in kind, and a fight started. The black man was getting beaten up by the off-duty, civilian-clothed officers when he escaped and ran into the street, calling, "Help," and "Police." An Executive Protective Service officer guarding a nearby embassy came on the scene ready to assist, but the off-duty police ran up saying, "Don't worry about it, we're cops." So now the EPS man jumped in to aid the officers in controlling the black guy.

Meanwhile someone had put in a call on the 911 emergency line. A sergeant and some officers drove up. The off-duty police identified themselves and assured their colleagues that there was no trouble. Believing the call had been false, the on-duty police left.

The black man, who must have been terrified at his inability to get help, took off running and made it to First District, where he finally got a patrolman to assist and protect him. But when he filed a complaint, the off-duty police tried to cover up their actions and get witnesses not to talk, making a bad situation worse. There were a lot of people involved, however, and the whole mess came out in no time. Criminally several of the men were charged with assault and obstructing justice. Administratively a number of them were fired.

Unfortunately this type of incident was not unique. Stories of off-duty police mistreating citizens surfaced a couple of times each year. However, the affair in the Irish bar, with its combination of racism and corruption of power, was the worst

I had heard of and more sinister than most. It occasioned several discussions between Gary and me about the relationship between police and society.

Gary and I both held the view that police officers ideally were and should be "the people in the middle." We meant this in both the literal and figurative senses. At a properly policed demonstration, the middle role was most visible. Lines of police officers stood physically between rival groups to prevent them from attacking each other or to arrest them if they tried.

Looked at more philosophically, the police role was to enforce the law and maintain an ordered society in which individuals had the maximum degree of freedom consistent with noninterference with others. The police should never identify with any one faction, although as individuals they should be recruited from as many different groups as possible so they can empathize with the problems of all factions. Where police abuses took over, officers usually were identifying with one side and treating the other as the enemy. Crusaders might provide exciting movie heroes, but they made dangerous law enforcers. The exemplary police attitude was summed up in the cliché we heard so often: "Hey, man, I've got nothing against you personally. I'm just doing my job."

Certainly there were instances where individuals betrayed their public trust. Yet in our experience, Gary and I found that most police officers could and did separate their personal prejudices from their official roles. It was sometimes quite remarkable and reassuring to see an officer whose private convictions we knew to be racist act impartially under all kinds of provocation while on duty.

One of the burdens a police officer lives with is that in a sense he is never off duty. In certain so-called off-duty circumstances, his obligations are clear. In a bar during an attempted holdup, he must identify himself as a police officer and act to thwart the criminal. Likewise, he may not invoke his official power because he objects to someone else who is peaceably and legally patronizing the establishment. But suppose an off-duty officer goes to a party and discovers that a fellow guest is smoking marijuana. Does the officer apologize to his host and arrest the guest?

Fortunately, because of the thoughtfulness of my hosts, I had never been placed in such a predicament. If I were, I'm not sure what I would do. I suspect I would simply leave, as long as I could exit before it became obvious to everyone that I was aware of what was going on. If, however, the violation and my knowledge of it were apparent, I would have to take action, and that would be very distasteful. Adding to the moral dilemma is the fact that what appears to be an "innocent" pot party among friends might be a setup by the Internal Affairs Division, with a detective watching to see how the officer acts. People in police work have to come to terms with a kind of separateness which the job imposes. I had mixed feelings about the action but tremendous sympathy for the predicament of an officer at Three D who locked up his girlfriend on a date when she lit up a "joint."

True reports, and also movies or books depicting police brutality or corruption, often evoked questions from our friends as to whether the police were "really like that?" Were things better in Washington than, say, New York or Chicago? If so, why? Gary and I would offer conjectures, and facts based on our experience. We could not speak for other cities, but in Washington, certain factors tended to minimize abuses by the police. The influence of Chief Jerry Wilson was felt strongly throughout the police community. He let it be known that he wanted fairness and would condemn all abuses. And the department was small enough so that he personally could be aware of and deal with a wide variety of problems.

As a city, D.C. was 72 percent black. Although somewhat less than half the police force was black, a bigoted white officer would not last long if he allowed his personal prejudice to come out on the job. Within the department itself, officers changed assignments frequently. There were very few permanent foot-beats that would give easy opportunities for payoffs. And since housing and health codes were not enforced by police anyway, there was actually very little a patrol officer could be paid to overlook.

Certainly bribes were given and taken. But a friend of ours in the U.S. Attorney's Office, where police, too, were prosecuted, told us he rarely saw cases involving uniformed patrol officers. "Vice squads are where the trouble is," he said. "We're investigating a number of police up to the rank of Inspector for allegedly having taken gambling payoffs."

The kinds of "gratuities" Gary and I heard about or experienced mainly involved restaurants giving free coffee and food. While I worked in Youth Division in my own clothes, the problem had never come up. As soon as I went on patrol in uniform, I found that not wanting to accept anything free was easier said than done. I walked into one sandwich shop for a cup of coffee. When I put a dollar bill on the counter, the man said, "No, that's okay," and moved away without taking the money. I had no change with me. While I could have left the dollar, I felt that was too high a price for a cup of coffee. But the incident bothered me and I talked to another sergeant. He told me that in that particular shop there was a cup for tips. He said he always left a tip equivalent to the cost of the coffee. The solution was fine as long as you had a quarter handy. I disliked accepting free food, but occasionally the only alternative was making a scene. In practice, I tried to stop at those places which allowed me to pay—and I tried to carry change with me besides.

"Wait a minute," I said. "Before we all just plow in, you tell *us* what we're looking for, too!"

Willis Darr, the officer I was questioning, had come on the air a couple of minutes earlier saying, "Hold me at 901 T Street for a turnup, and send me a backup unit." A turnup meant a planned arrest.

I had been riding in a scout car with a new man in my squad because I didn't have a cruiser that day. The dispatcher assigned my scout as the backup. I advised that we were responding and had an official aboard. A detective got on the radio to say he was also responding.

Darr, who had been waiting for us at the scene, said, "We're looking for a guy named Snake." He didn't have much of a description, except that the subject was a male Negro, dark complexion, fairly large. He was wanted for robbery, force and violence. The officer had just left his partner with the complainant at the hospital. Snake was supposed to live on the second floor at 901 T Street.

The four of us—two officers, the detective and me—went into the three-story building together. We got to what we considered the second floor—it was the middle one—and nobody around claimed to be Snake or to know of any such person. But we had blown it, because there we were, three of us in uniform, saying "Who's Snake?" Obviously no one was going to speak up.

Then Darr made a smart move. He was black, and his voice sounded black. Not identifying himself as police, he started up the stairs hollering, "Snake? Hey, Snake, where are you?"

And a voice from above said, "I'm in here!"

Great. We all raced up. Standing in an open apartment doorway was a huge black man with a shaved head. The minute he saw the first uniform he knew he'd been had. He took a step back into his apartment, but at that point he couldn't very well deny who he was. He was the only one up there and he had just acknowledged to the name "Snake."

The two officers stepped forward and the one who knew the situation started to question him. Where had he been an hour earlier? Did he know such and such a person? Nah. Had they had a fight? No.

I glanced at the detective. Both officers were being indecisive by not moving right in to arrest the man, who had answered to the right name and been in the designated building. As they talked, Snake began to object. He backed a little farther into the room, drawing them forward. He was looking around, shifting slightly on the balls of his feet. Then the officer I had been riding with said, "I'm sorry, sir, but we're going to have to put handcuffs on you." Instead of just doing it!

At that, even as the officers reached for his wrists, Snake *threw* up his arms, caught both officers across the chest and started fighting them. The man was really big, and the two officers—one tall, skinny and weak, the other shorter, fat and also weak—couldn't even control one arm apiece.

The detective and I went through the doorway yelling, "Turn him around." Because here were these two officers between us and the suspect so we couldn't help until we got an angle on him. The officers managed to sidestep Snake so his back was toward us, but Snake was still having no trouble handling the two of them. He pushed and they went back against a wall. A table skidded sideways and a chair went flying. Snake had the two cops pinned against the wall, one hand on each officer's chest, when the detective and I grabbed his arms from behind. That released the officers. With four to one, Snake didn't really have a chance, but he still put up a fight and I felt a crack on the bridge of my nose as my glasses got knocked off. The detective had his handcuffs out first. Controlling Snake's one arm with one hand, he slapped a cuff open against Snake's wristbone. I was holding onto Snake's other arm with both hands. I pulled his remaining free wrist back and the detective snapped the second handcuff onto it.

"Those fuckin' things are breaking my wrists," yelled Snake when we finally had him. We had wasted no time double-locking them, and Snake's twisting just made them get tighter.

We read Snake his rights. Darr and the officer I had been riding with took him to the station. I went with the detective to Freedmen's Hospital, where the complainant was. We were eager to verify Snake's identity, because we had had an inadequate description of him to start with, and the nickname was not that uncommon. If by chance the complainant did not corroborate that we had the right man, we wanted to get him released. We could in a sense "unarrest" him by putting him on what we called a detention journal. This was a D.C. system that gave us a couple of hours after making an arrest on probable cause to check out a suspect's alibi. If we discovered that we had the wrong person, we didn't have to make it worse by holding him overnight to go see a judge. We just eliminated his name from the public arrest book but recorded it on the nonpublic detention journal so that we weren't making our arrest a secret. Furthermore, the subject was given legal forms stating that he had the right to say he had not been arrested if he was asked about it sometime in the future—when filling in a job application, for example.

The questioning at the hospital was very unsatisfying. The complainant, who turned out to have some broken ribs, was either not very intelligent, dazed, or simply unwilling to cooperate. He still could or would not give us a good description. The most obvious thing for him to have noticed was that his assailant had a shaved head, but he never mentioned it. He just kept saying he was big. And he claimed to know him only by his nickname.

We returned to the station uncertain about whether we should hold our subject for a court hearing. At Three D, however, we found the situation had been resolved. Snake had confessed to part of the charge. He admitted having gotten into a fight with the complainant but denied robbing him of any money.

The case went to court the next morning. I learned later that they had no-papered it, which meant they dropped the charges in court. The complainant declined to prosecute. We would never know whether it was because he shared responsibility for the fight or was just too afraid of Snake.

Obviously this kind of ending was a letdown. Officers experienced it more often than officials, because we seldom went to court or learned the outcome of cases. Yet I could find some satisfaction in knowing I had done my job.

The five-minute episode—that's all the time it took from when we ran up the stairs to when we had Snake under control—had again left my muscles tensed and shaking. But what I found interesting was that, in this case at least, my own strength had apparently been as great as that of either officer's.

* * *

I was driving on the Strip Saturday night when a white Mercedes-Benz came up behind me, honking. I pulled over, wondering whether something was the matter with my car, or whether *I* had done anything wrong. Police are people, too.

A fairly distinguished-looking white man in a topcoat came popping out of the Mercedes and over to my cruiser. He certainly wasn't a typical Fourteenth Street habitué. As he reached the window of my car, he did a double-take at seeing a woman behind the wheel, but then he blurted out anyway, "I've just been had!"

"What do you mean?"

"She stole my wallet."

"Exactly what happened, sir?"

He opened his mouth as if he was about to give me some line and then seemed to decide he might as well tell me the real story. "I met this prostitute—very high-class prostitute, I might say—at a very nice place downtown. I was taking her home, and she directed me to an alley back there. I don't remember the name but I can point it out to you."

And I was thinking, "Yeah, sure, what high-class prostitute brings a guy to an alley around Euclid Street, Northwest?"

This citizen then went on to tell me how she got him "distracted" and then took his wallet and ran. He was some kind of upset. He was also obnoxious. In between telling me the facts, he was trying to impress me. He was an international lawyer and he had been in cities in Europe and Japan and the Near East—one got the impression he had been whoring all over the world—and he was very experienced and this was the first time he had ever been had. "I suppose maybe it was my turn," he concluded.

"Well, sir, what do you want us to do?" This didn't seem like a man who would want his name in the newspaper the next day as a result of making a police report.

He thought for a minute and said that one thing he definitely wanted was for the police to accompany him back to the alley to see whether the wallet had been discarded, because it wasn't his money he was so concerned about, but all his credit cards.

I said, "Fine. I'll call a scout car and we can go back with our spotlights and check the alleys."

I radioed the dispatcher.

Meanwhile, the man said he supposed he had to make a report if his wallet wasn't found because he had to cover the loss of the credit cards. He didn't seem particularly fazed by the potential embarrassment. He was looking at me and suddenly, quite pleasantly, he asked, "Are you studying law?" Out of the blue. I mean, how many police officers were apt to be studying law?

"Well, yes, as a matter of fact."

"Oh. Do you study at Georgetown?"

"Yes, I do!"

Then he asked if I knew a certain professor.

"I'm taking his course!"

"Oh, well, he's a real good friend of mine," said this man. "You be sure next time you see him to say that you met me and I said hello."

And I was thinking to myself, "This guy has got to be out of his mind." Not only was he telling me all about himself when he should probably want to remain anonymous, but what was I supposed to do? Go up to the professor and say, "I'm a police officer and I was on Fourteenth Street the other night and I've got greetings from a friend of yours who got robbed by a prostitute"?

The scout car I had called for came, together with a detective cruiser. There was a long discussion as the lawyer described the prostitute in question, and then went to search the alley.

No wallet was found. The lawyer decided he did not want to make a full complaint but simply wanted it to be a lost-wallet report. The officers took the information and started to make the report. The lawyer returned to his car, but was back in a minute. He had just *found* his wallet lying right on the back seat of his car. Now there were more questions, because this man had given us the impression that he and the prostitute were out of the car and in the alley, but in fact they had both been in his back seat. The prostitute had taken the money but left the wallet and credit cards. So he wanted no report at all. The lawyer said he would chalk it up to experience, and he returned to his car and drove away.

The detectives, meanwhile, were mumbling together. Finally they told the rest of us what they had been discussing. Based on the bit about the back seat, where our lawyer had probably been promised a quick blow job, and based on his description of the prostitute, it was the detectives' opinion that "she" had not been a woman in the first place. Our worldly lawyer got taken by a female impersonator!

17

BAG CASE

TO ALL MEMBERS OF THE THIRD DISTRICT:

It has been brought to the attention of the Inspector that there has been excessive use of foul and abusive language in the exchange of normal verbal intercourse in the station. In order to alleviate this horrendous situation and at the same time not interfere with individual freedom and originality, the following code numbers shall be uttered in lieu of the catchy phrases listed beside each number:

101—You've got to be shitting me
102—Get off my fucking back
103—Beats the shit out of me
104—What the fuck
105—It's so fucking bad I can't believe it
106—I hate this fucking place
107—This place sucks
108—Fuck you very much
109—Lovely, simply fucking lovely
110—Bite my bippy
111—Beautiful, just fucking beautiful
112—Fuck, shit, piss
113—Hair pie, fur burgers
114—I just got fucked
115—Big fucking deal
116—Hang it in your fucking ear
117—Get bent
118—I don't give a shit

119—You've got fucking balls
120—Merry fucking Christmas
121—Fuck it, just fuck it
122—Hot shit
123—Bitch, bitch, bitch
124—Tell someone who gives a shit
125—Don't get fucking wise
126—I don't give a fuck
127—Pardon me, sir. You obviously mistook me for someone who gives a fuck
128—Your ass sucks wind
129—Satchel ass
130—Go pound sand in your ass
131—Shut your fucking mouth
132—Shit head
133—It's not worth a good fuck
134—That really pisses me off
135—Smart ass
136—What's this shit

230

Copies of the memo were handed out, and for about a week, the codes were used with glee.

Lieutenant Lewis had been promoted and transferred to Criminal Investigations Division. One night his replacement, Lieutenant Bennet, said to me, "Sergeant Abrecht, were *you* working this tour?"

I stopped dead. "Have you been talking to Lieutenant Lewis by any chance?"

"As a matter of fact, I saw Lewis at a meeting a couple of days ago, and I told him you'd been looking a lot happier since he'd left. He said maybe I ought to start pestering you more because it wasn't good for a sergeant to be too happy!"

After that, I took the lieutenant's occasional remarks as kidding, and they no longer bothered me.

I had two new men in my squad. Because mine was one of the more junior squads, there was a relatively high turnover as officers filled openings in senior squads with better cars and days off. One of the new men lodged a complaint that his male partner did not back him up.

The incident precipitating the complaint happened one shift while the pair was riding the wagon. They were heading down a one-way street when they saw a man who was walking in the opposite direction stuff something under his coat. The driver, Mills, said he thought it looked like a rifle, and he slammed on his brakes, jumped out and gave chase on foot after the man, who took off running.

Stafford, the officer now left in the passenger's seat, felt that the last thing to do was give chase on foot, especially without notifying the dispatcher. The big radio console was between him and the driver's seat. He ran around the front of the vehicle, jumped in and turned the wagon around. As he drove in pursuit, he got on the radio to advise that his partner was chasing a man who possibly had a gun and he gave the direction in which they were heading.

Given a choice of things to do, Stafford's conduct was reasonable and could not be interpreted as "chicken." He was certainly acting responsibly by informing others of what was happening and where. Pursuit in the wagon, while causing a temporary delay, would have given him the advantage in a lengthy chase. On the other hand, if his partner had gotten into immediate trouble, Stafford would not have been there to help. Under the circumstances, Stafford could have used the radio from his own seat and then been more aggressive in following Mills on foot.

Mills insisted that the only proper move would have been for his partner to jump out on foot right behind him, regardless of whether the dispatcher knew where they were. The suspicious man had not been caught, but Mills said flatly, "My partner wasn't there when I needed him. I don't want to work with him again. He doesn't back you up."

The case was a standoff between men with opposite approaches to a problem. Lieutenant Bennet and I handled it as a counseling situation, pointing out the alternative actions that had been possible. Then, with everybody present, Bennet spoke forcefully to each man in turn.

"Stafford, right or wrong, you gave Mills the impression you weren't backing him up. I know you're quiet, and I think you're level-headed. I'm not convinced you were afraid. But you have to convince Mills that you'll be there to back him up in the future. I don't intend to let this episode get blown out of proportion, but if there is anything to what Mills is saying, we don't want you on the force."

Bennet turned to Mills. "Okay, you're a hot shot and you know you're impulsive. Well, when you begin working with a new partner, you've got to get certain things understood between you. You can't just jump out of a car and think he's going to know what's in your head. If you feel so strongly that you never want your partner to stop and notify the dispatcher, you at least owe it to him to tell him that.

"You guys know you can't always pick and choose your partners. On this force, every officer has to be ready, willing and able to help and depend on every other officer. That's how we work."

Winter arrived, and getting ready for an eight-hour tour involved much more clothing: earmuffs, mufflers, ski underwear, heavy socks. Because I had had difficulty the previous year in finding suitable gloves on sale after Christmas, I had decided to order several sets of sturdy, warm gloves well ahead of the season from the Sears catalog. Gary had been interested in doing the same thing, since his hands, like mine, are larger than average. Looking through the catalog together, we found that the manufacturers of this world really discriminate against women in terms of helping them prepare for a job like mine. We opened to the glove section. On the women's side, the Sears catalog talked about the soft leather and fine detail of their lovely, attractive gloves. On the men's side, it was all sturdy construction and thermal lining to keep your hands warm. The products that arrived mimicked the ads. I had already gone through my first pair of gloves, which just didn't hold up under rough wear. And my hands were seldom warm when I was out of the car.

I was working a Sunday day tour in January, 1974, the only sergeant on duty in my platoon. I had one of my senior officers as an acting sergeant. I drove around for many quiet hours. It had snowed the night before, and the sunlight was reflecting brilliantly from the sidewalks and small yards where the slush had not yet taken over.

About 2 P.M. a call came out for Scout 89 and any official, an unconscious person at such and such an address. From the way the call came, I had a hunch it was a dead person. First of all, they weren't bothering to send an ambulance. Also, the dispatcher had requested an official from the start.

I acknowledged the call and drove to the address, which was a five-story building on Vernon Street. The scout car was there, but no officers were in sight.

I opened the downstairs door of the apartment building and immediately smelled a strange odor. I still couldn't see any police, so I just kind of followed the odor, which became increasingly unpleasant. It was strongest in front of one particular door at a small, raised landing on the first floor of the building.

I was about to knock when another door down the hallway opened, and Officer Ollie stepped out. He was the policeman who had been cut behind the ear. He told me the corpse was in the apartment in front of me, but he hadn't been inside yet. The sister and brother-in-law of the dead man had discovered the body and called the police. The couple were in the neighbor's apartment Ollie had just left. Ollie reported they had last seen their relative the previous Tuesday, when he visited and had dinner with them. He had not shown up at work the next day, and had not been seen or heard of since, so possibly he had died shortly after returning home Tuesday night. In any case, it was not until today, five days later, that the sister and brother-in-law had had some free time to come check on him. When they arrived and rang his doorbell, there was no answer. Even before the door was opened for the first time, the brother-in-law thought he recognized a faint odor and had an idea of what they would find. They checked the mail room and his mail was stacked up in the box. Then they got the janitor to let them in.

The instant the door was opened, the smell hit them. The janitor took off like a shot. The sister never entered. The brother-in-law walked in, found the body and left immediately.

"I guess it's a pretty gross scene," Officer Ollie said. "The guy told me his brother-in-law died sitting on the john."

"We better take a look around before we call Homicide. Are you working alone?" Ollie nodded. "Why don't you get the brother-in-law out here?"

Ollie returned in a moment with the man.

"Sir, we have to go inside and take a preliminary look around, and it would be best if a relative was with us while we checked for valuables and things."

The man shook his head. "I'd rather not go back in there."

"But if there's money lying around—or personal papers— a relative really should be present."

The man backed away. "It's okay, I trust you. Really, I just don't want to go back in." He looked at me and suddenly seemed to realize I was a woman. He said to Officer Ollie, "It's terrible in there."

Ollie glanced at me. I felt sorry for the relative and didn't want to push him. "Why don't you just direct us to where the body is?"

He gave the slightest nod and opened the door to the most nauseating odor I had ever smelled. We took a few steps into a narrow foyer. The heat was on in the apartment, and the stink was like nothing else on earth, much more foul and infectious-seeming than a rotting animal. I had read it described as "cabbagelike." It was just overwhelmingly vile and indescribable.

"He's in the bathroom—down at the end, where the hallway turns to the left. I'm going back to my wife now." The man left.

Officer Ollie and I went along the foyer. The overhead light was on. We turned left. The bathroom light was also on, and the door was open. We stopped in the doorway and stared at a body seated with its pants down on the john. It was bloated to a point where it hardly looked human. The head tilted against one shoulder and was swollen to twice a normal size. There was no way of telling how large this man had been to start with, but because of his position, his thighs were grotesque and lapped over the seat of the toilet. It took me a moment to recognize that a huge, almost round object aimed straight at us was his swollen penis.

I just gulped. Officer Ollie said, "Jesus Christ."

Because the man had died in a small, overheated room, it was as though he had died in the hottest summer weather. The swelling was from gasses caused by bacteria.

We didn't stand there for long because the smell was overwhelming. I closed the door behind us. We tried to open some windows but they all seemed to be painted shut. "Let's take a quick look around."

Without a relative present, it was difficult to know whether anything was missing. Evidence of a theft can be important because it may suggest a motive for murder. In this case, the man seemed to have had very little. A portable TV was still sitting on a table in the living room. His wallet with some money and a couple of credit cards was on the bedroom bureau. I had a slightly odd, snooping feeling going through this apartment while its dead owner was in the bathroom. We looked for things like bottles of pills and signs of a last meal in case there was anything strange about that. I did find some papers with a doctor's name on them. Apparently the dead man was being treated for both diabetes and heart disease.

"We may as well call Homicide." I used the phone in the bedroom.

The Homicide detective arrived quickly. He was deadpan and didn't comment on the odor in the foyer. Homicide had to go to scenes like this all the time, and they studied being cool. We led him back to the bathroom. He took one look at the enormous penis pointing straight out. "I hope it doesn't go off." Both Officer Ollie and I were trying to be cool, but I guess it was apparent that we were thoroughly grossed out. The detective stared pointedly at the penis. "No different from looking down the barrel of a forty-five."

Still Officer Ollie and I refused to react. Finally, in recognition of the smell, the detective said, "One of these days I'm going to take up cigars." A lot of Homicide and morgue men came to scenes puffing cigars or smoking pipes filled with the most god-awful tobacco they could find to try to kill the body's stink.

The detective searched the apartment but found nothing we hadn't. I gave him the medical papers and he telephoned the man's doctor. Afterward he commented that a sick body deteriorates faster than a healthy one. He went out briefly to his car to call for the morgue wagon. As usual, there was a considerable wait for it to arrive. The detective nodded in the direction of the bathroom. "I hope he doesn't pop before those guys get here."

The thought that the body might literally blow up had already occurred to me. It was one of the things frequently mentioned in stories about scenes like this. I asked what it was like when the body did explode. The detective answered in terms of how it affected his work. "It's a mess because it's so difficult to determine cause of death. You walk in and it looks like it was absolute mayhem. There's blood and guts all over the walls, so then you have to get an autopsy with a really careful analysis of every portion to decide whether some hole in the leg was a gunshot wound or where the leg exploded."

We talked a little more, about homicides and things in general, while we waited for the wagon. That was Officer Ollie's chance to tell me how they had closed his cutting case. We had been on the scene for nearly an hour. Ollie kidded about how he hoped his 3 p.m. checkoff time would come before the morgue wagon because this was one case he would love to turn over to his relief. "Except I want to be here to see the guy's face," he added.

I went out to my cruiser to see what was going on. I still had a little over an hour before my tour ended at four, and if I was needed elsewhere, there was no reason I had to stay on this scene. Also, I was glad to get a breath of fresh air.

Sitting in my car for a minute, I was aware of how different my reaction as a police officer was from the way I would probably have felt if, as a private citizen, off duty, I had walked into an apartment and found someone I knew dead. I might have gone to pieces. But this afternoon when the call had come out, I had had time to prepare for the idea that

I would probably find a dead body. The unexpected things were the guy being on the john and having been dead for a while. Yet I was on the scene as a police officer. Facing the situation in the context of my job made a great difference. There was a certain attitude you took on when you dressed in your uniform and started work on a given day. It helped carry you through to the end of your tour.

I was heading back into the building when the white van with the D.C. Medical Examiner's sign on the door pulled up. Next thing I knew, two dudes straight out of *Superfly* got out of the morgue wagon. They were just the craziest-looking couple of characters. They both wore big hats and flashy clothes. One of them had a three-quarter-length suede coat on and was really dressed to kill. I thought, "Wait until he sees that body. He's going to take off that suede coat *so* fast . . ."

I led them to the apartment. One of them sniffed knowingly. "Hmm, who's cookin' what?"

"The body's in there." I pointed. The hallway was narrow. Officer Ollie and the detective were already at the end where the bathroom was, and since there wasn't room for all of us to gather and have a view, I motioned the morgue guys to go on ahead of me. Their first reaction at seeing the body was to turn, stare at me, look at the Homicide detective and say, "Did *she* see this?"

At which point I managed a casual, "Sure. What's the problem?"

Both men turned on their heels, departed and were back in a minute, the one minus his suede coat, both missing their big hats and with lab coats covering their own clothes.

"You all gonna help us carry him out?" they asked pleasantly.

They were just testing our reactions with the standard

trick they always played on rookies. This body was much too far gone to even try to load onto a stretcher.

The morgue men unzipped a large, dark green rubber bag and took it into the bathroom. They first covered the body with part of the bag and then, moving carefully but quickly, they enveloped the body and sealed it inside. There was little doubt that as soon as the pressure of the bag being lifted hit the body, the dead man would split apart.

One of the worst sights of all was the body leaving. I followed the morgue people out. As they went down the stairs, being careful so they wouldn't slip on the ice, I could see by the slow, easy movement of the bag's contents that the object inside was no longer a firm human being. The bottom of the bag hung heavy and formless. You could practically feel the sloshing within.

Officer Ollie had gotten the names of the morgue men for the death report he still had to write before checking off. The circumstances of the death had to be described, and as always, all officers and officials present on the scene had to be listed. Before leaving, Ollie told me this bag case was the worst of the dead ones he had been on in his two years with the force. The detective volunteered the information that the bags were reusable, which struck me as preposterous because I couldn't imagine who would wash them out. He didn't know. We left the apartment in charge of the relatives.

I got back in my cruiser with nearly an hour to go before my checkoff. I wasn't sure whether the odor I continued to smell was in my clothes or my nostrils. The Homicide detective had said he had left his heavy winter coat in his car because he knew from my call what he was going to find. "And if I hadn't, I'd have taken it off as soon as I hit the front door. You get a bitch of a cleaning bill otherwise, because if you wear a coat into one of these things, that's the last time you have it on until it goes to the cleaners."

The smell permeates everything, and I felt sure if I had just walked outside into a warm summer day, it would have been ten times worse. As it happened, there was a cold breeze and a light snow starting to fall again, and they were refreshing.

My last hour on tour went quietly. I kept thinking, "Well. So I've been there for my first funky dead one. Good."

I went home, showered, washed my hair and changed clothes. I fixed a spaghetti dinner for Gary and me. We were just starting to eat when suddenly, for the first time, I felt really nauseated. I pushed my plate away and left the table.

I studied a little for one of my law courses, but later in the evening when I didn't have anything in particular to do, the flashbacks I got, both of smell and sight, were worse than the actual scene.

Gary sympathized. He said that even a small whiff of that particular odor was absolutely nauseating to him and really made him want to upchuck. But there was no question in my mind that the grossest part of the whole thing had not been the smell but the sight of that penis. I teased Gary, "Better not get too close to me. I'm not sure I ever want to see a man again. And whatever you do, don't ever die on the john!"

18

CHANGES

"I don't think you could stand it in the U.S. Attorney's Office," Gary said. "They're just too straight."

"Maybe."

I had been telling Gary about some kidding that had gone on at the station. I still wasn't part of the men's locker room conversation or their after-work beer drinking, but for some time, they had been much more relaxed at my being around.

That didn't mean a bunch of them wouldn't stop a conversation as I approached. Once when this happened, Sergeant Lacy said, "Now, you know this really isn't fair. Here we're all exchanging phone numbers and nobody ever remembers poor Mary. I think we should help her out too. Let's get her a couple of names and numbers."

And Bennet said, "Well, she's got my phone number but she never uses it."

At that point I was standing in front of the coffee machine. Bennet passed over fifteen cents for the collection can, so of course I just looked and said, "For fifteen cents, Bennet, what do you expect?"

Routines like that were simply part of the largely male environment. You heard the same thing going on with the homeliest sixty-five-year-old female records clerk. It had been different when I was first on the department before Gary joined or before it was widely known that I had a police husband and therefore was not fair game. Then, there was little public kidding and more direct invitations to go out on a date. If I answered that I was married, I would often hear, "Well, that doesn't bother me. Does it bother you?"

There was in fact a lot of fooling around, both by married as well as single men. Most of them didn't try to hide it. In the sergeants' room an official going off duty would say to someone coming onto the next shift, "If my wife calls, I'm working late." Some of the men would laugh a little obscenely and go along with it. Others would say, "The hell with you. If your wife calls, I'll tell her you checked off at midnight. If you can't cover up your own business, don't ask me to."

There were standard in-jokes related to the job. Anytime someone had the slightest accident—like tripping, or bumping his knee on a desk or dropping something on his foot—he would turn on the nearest person. "Okay, you saw that. You're my witness, right?" Implying he was going to put in for disability retirement.

Often one bit would lead to another as the men egged each other on. Obscenity was pervasive, either because it was a man's personal style or his view of what was appropriate in the male ambiance. Gary told me my own language was beginning to show signs of police influence.

During revolver inspection, which was held once a week on Saturday, an officer said to another, "My God, why doncha clean that piece? Your barrel is as dirty as my asshole."

I glared at them and answered, "Well, a wire brush and a little solvent would take care of both your problems."

There was no doubt that the atmosphere in the U.S. Attorney's Office would be entirely different. There was also no question that the law was becoming more important to me. A growing number of my friends outside work were lawyers or law students.

More important, I enjoyed and was stimulated by the legal questions that arose when Gary and I had bull sessions with a mixed group of police and lawyers we had gotten to know. I walked in on one of these discussions about the legality of searches, where my reaction was distinctly different from what it would have been before I had become a patrol sergeant.

There was a controversy in D.C. as to whether you could search in a traffic stop situation. One particular case drew the line of battle clearly. It involved a man arrested for a traffic offense, discovered to be carrying narcotics in a package of cigarettes. The question was, was this search reasonable when the arrest was for a traffic violation?

Normally, police in D.C. did not search the driver during a routine traffic stop, although we did look around enough to make sure there was no weapon visible or in an unlocked glove compartment within easy reach. If the driver got out of his car, the officers might frisk him to be sure he did not have a weapon he was going to draw during the confrontation. If, however, the person was guilty of a serious traffic offense requiring a full-custody arrest (taking him to the station-house), he would be searched at the scene to insure safety and security during transport. He and any objects in his possession would then be searched more thoroughly at the station.

Many liberals regarded this treatment as an invasion of privacy and a means of picking on certain types of subjects. They accused police of arresting people on flimsy traffic charges as an excuse to search them for evidence of other crimes.

I arrived in the middle of such an argument the day after

my wagon men told me about a situation in which they almost got themselves hurt. They had arrested a man on whom a string of traffic warrants was outstanding. After checking him quickly at the scene, they brought him to the station. While they were processing him, they saw him put his thumb down on the table and slip off a paperclip. He casually picked his teeth with it for a minute, and then it disappeared. It had obviously gone into his mouth. A paperclip. Just something they noticed but didn't act on immediately.

A little later, when they searched him, they had him take off his shoes. They examined one shoe carefully, but were momentarily distracted as he removed the other, so they didn't really look at it. They did recognize that he was very quick to put his foot back into it, so they recovered themselves and said, "Take that second shoe off again." He started to fudge. They grabbed him and forced the shoe off. He had a knife in it.

Having been discovered, the defendant came out with the whole story. He quite simply had his escape planned. The paperclip was to undo the handcuffs. The handcuff-locking mechanism is a very simple one which can be manipulated without a key. Then, he said, he was going to jump them with the knife and get away. The officers felt that only their thoroughness in searching had kept them safe.

In the 1973 case of *United States v. W. Robinson, Jr.*, the Supreme Court held that the police had acted properly in searching the cigarette package. I agreed with the Court's decision. Although narcotics were found, the package might equally well have contained a razor blade or some other item which could have been used offensively by the prisoner.

But in one of our discussion groups, I raised what to me was a more difficult problem. Granted the Court's decision, where did one draw the line? I told of once having unwittingly subjected a female traffic violator to a full narcotics strip search. I still felt this had been a clear invasion of privacy. The woman was being temporarily detained, not jailed overnight. My search had gone the whole way, including making her bend over, separate her buttocks and present a view of her vagina. Surely even the most conservative legal mind would agree that if a weapon were somehow hidden internally, it was certainly not easily accessible. The element of danger was remote.

Yet I had been taught that when I was called to the police station to search a woman, it was by definition a strip search. Of course there were degrees of strip searches. The one for weapons was less intimate. But was even that proper? As a police officer, I saw men being searched in the open, at the counter, by a thorough patdown, emptying of their pockets and removal of shoes or boots. It seemed to me that only rarely did I see male officers take prisoners into the men's room to remove all their clothes. Were women prisoners being treated more stringently? I didn't know the answer.

Early in 1974, I submitted a formal application to join the staff of the U.S. Attorney's Office. After a series of interviews, I received in April a letter of acceptance dependent on a number of contingencies. First, I obviously had to be graduated from law school (that would be in June) and pass the bar exam. The exams were given the end of July. The results would not come out until December. If I passed, I would still have to undergo a security check by the FBI and wait for a vacancy in the U.S. Attorney's Office. By the time the transfer was final, it was likely to be the middle of 1975. While the acceptance was enormously gratifying, all these plans seemed far in the future.

Meanwhile, my police job was more interesting than ever. For one thing, I had changed. On a quiet tour, I no longer felt I was missing all the action. I knew that during any given shift in a particular area, very little might be going on.

On slow nights I found myself wishing something would happen. If a call came out for a shooting, I would think, "I hope that's a good one." Meaning someone got hit, as opposed to someone hearing firecrackers. Because that was my job. Obviously, if there was no crime, there would be no job. Yet just as obviously, this was a peculiar police mentality, because in an ideal world, police would be unnecessary. I thought perhaps the need to demonstrate or even create their own necessity played a role in the way certain officers seemed to encourage physical violence by their own rough handling of subjects.

Female officers I came in contact with often mentioned that they were spending much more of their time helping people than they had expected. Occasionally they were indignant that men for so long had protected their domain by exaggerating the dangers and difficulties of their jobs. Doing so was certainly to their advantage not only in keeping the women out but in gaining higher pay and better benefits. Much of police work does turn out to be routine. However, any situation has the potential for sudden violence. Every officer has to live with that reality.

I liked working alone, being free to handle things in my own style. I had enough street hours behind me both to gain a degree of confidence and to realize that experience alone was no guarantee of good performance. Usually the individual's on-the-spot judgment was more important than his having been at a dozen similar scenes. Because each situation was new and different in its own way.

One Sunday morning I expedited to two gun calls in a

row. The first time, I hadn't been on the street more than ten minutes when a run came out for shots being fired. I raced in with my red light and siren going, to an address in the 1400 block of Swann Street, Northwest. Two scout cars arrived almost simultaneously.

Four officers and I lined up against the wall on each side of the entrance to the building, our guns in our hands. We knocked and finally an old man and woman opened the door together. We explained that we had gotten a call for a shooting at this address.

"We didn't call the police. There was no shooting here."

Then we had that awkward moment of deciding whether to leave or check further. Obviously if there was a shooting in your house and you had anything to do with it, you weren't going to volunteer the information to the police. "Do you mind if we look around?" I asked.

"Go ahead."

We checked the entire first floor and found nothing. As we started up the stairs, I asked whether anyone was above. After all, it was early Sunday morning and I didn't want to scare some innocent person half to death. The old woman told us her nephew was sleeping upstairs. By now we were all pretty well convinced this was a false alarm.

We went up anyway. Several of the doors had padlocks on them, and we passed these by. One door was slightly ajar. We opened it up, and there was a man lying on the floor next to the bed. We all just looked at each other. I thought, "Well, we certainly did the right thing coming up here after all." It seemed pretty clear this man wasn't just asleep for the night, not when he was sprawled on the floor with a perfectly good bed right there.

Two of the officers watched the hallway while three of us moved closer, looking for a wound or signs of blood. But there was nothing. And the guy was snoring lightly.

I touched his shoulder. He mumbled groggily. I pushed harder and suddenly he awoke to a bedroom full of uniformed police. "What is it? What's going on?"

"It's all right, sir. We're just checking. Have you been shot?"

"Whaatt? No, I haven't been shot."

"Then you're okay, sir?"

"Yeah, I'm okay. I'm just sleepy." And he rolled onto his side and went back to sleep.

We went downstairs and bid the elderly couple farewell. "By the way, ma'am, your nephew is sleeping on the floor of his room."

The old woman nodded. "Says it's a whole lot better for his back. Says we got to get a board to put in his bed." She followed us outside. "Says the doctor told him that would help." We were starting down the stairs. "Says boards don't cost much. But I don't know."

The second call was given to my two wagon officers—one male, one female—and me. All scout cars were out of service on other assignments. I pulled up first but before I had turned off my engine, the patrol wagon came barreling up behind me, looming into my rear-view mirror as it jerked to a stop about an inch from my back bumper. As I got out of my cruiser, the wagon's driver, Officer Joan Michaels, jumped down from her high seat and tore past me. Her partner and I raced after her into the building. While her partner followed her upstairs, I went into a front room, which seemed to be a rental office. There were a couple of people inside and a man seated behind a desk.

"We've had a call that somebody here has a gun. Do you know anything about it?" I asked the group as a whole.

"Yeah, I've got a gun," said the man at the desk. "It's in this drawer right here, but it's registered."

"Oh. Well, let's see it."

He pulled open the drawer and lifted out a holstered gun, holding it with two fingers and watching me all the time. He placed the weapon on his desk and showed me the registration papers, explaining that he kept the gun in his office and it was all perfectly legal.

What interested me at that point was the *way* he had his weapon—in a holster on a gun belt. A citizen was permitted to have a gun registered for a place of business or a residence, but he was *not* allowed to carry it loaded on a belt between home and work. I explained to the man that the only way he could legally carry that gun on the street was unloaded and securely wrapped. The two wagon officers came into the room as I continued. "Sir, you do understand that someone was aware of your having this gun and sufficiently worried to call the police." Officer Joan Michaels had walked up to the desk, glanced at the registration papers and was examining the gun's grips with interest. The man's attention alternated between her and me. I said, "I suggest, sir, that from now on, you be especially careful about where you keep your weapon and—"

Michaels interrupted. "What the sarge is trying to say, mister, is that if we ever catch your ass on the street wearing this"—she hefted the gun under his nose—"you're gonna get yourself busted." She shoved the gun back into the holster and dropped the whole thing noisily on his desk.

The man sat motionless. The others in the office stared. "Sorry if we caused you any trouble, sir," I said as we left.

"Watch your step, mister, 'cause there's others will be watching it too," Michaels threw over her shoulder. Outside she added, "Sarge, I know that building. We get a lot of trouble there. That guy's got to be up to something. I guarantee we'll catch him dirty one of these times."

Officer Michaels was one of the "new women." She had

joined the force after females were routinely being given patrol training and assignment. She had a high school education, an almost instinctive street sense and a gusto for her work. In the old days, she would never have been given the chance to use her talents on the force. Now she was more typical of female officers than I was.

Obviously she was not going to have the same problems I had encountered when I went on patrol. The action aspect of street work came naturally to her. Subtleties, explanations and public relations didn't interest her. She just got on with the job. I, on the other hand, liked to study a situation, explain it to a citizen, citing chapter and verse of the law if necessary, and have all the loose ends neatly tied up before I let a matter drop. I thought there was room for both types of personalities on the force.

In the spring of 1974, I was given a senior squad, Cruiser 242 and Sunday and Monday as my days off. For the first time since Personnel, I had half the weekend free. Gary still wasn't senior enough to rate that. We were, however, on the same two-week rotation schedule—evening, morning, midnight —so at least we kept the same hours.

19

SECOND SUMMER

My second summer as a patrol sergeant began. Again I anticipated increased problems for the police, yet having been through it once made a difference.

I was working an evening tour in June when a call came out for a burglary in progress. I was fairly close, flipped on my siren and arrived first on the scene. The address was a medium-sized apartment building. Probably it was not a good idea to go in before the backup units came. But a burglary in progress. I hated to stand around waiting because, my God, I might be able to stop something. On TV, police are always walking in on serious crimes as they are happening. In real life this is a rare occurrence.

I ran into the building, got up to the apartment where the break-in was supposed to be occurring and knocked. A couple of kids came to the door.

"Did someone here call the police?"

"Yeah. Mommy called. She's up with the resident manager and he's there too."

"Who's 'he'?"

The children explained that a friend of their mother's wanted to see them, but there was something wrong with him and the mother wouldn't let him in. They said the man had gone up to talk to the resident manager (about getting a passkey, I figured) and Mother had gone up after him.

I found the resident manager's apartment, where the mother told me the man had been trying to break into her place. The man shouted they were his kids he wanted to see. So our burglary in progress was turning out to be a family dispute. The only thing that made it unusual was that when I had the man step out of the manager's apartment so we could talk, he kept moving in on me. He was definitely strange-looking, probably strung out on something, and as we conversed, he kept advancing, talking about an inch in front of my face.

So there I was with the freaky guy, whose wife was afraid of him, backing up while he kept moving in on me, talking all the time. "Look, I don't want any trouble, but get this straight." His voice was loud and strained. "That's my *wife* in there and I've got every right to see my kids, so don't mess with me." Meanwhile he was moving me all around the floor.

I had my nightstick with me, and I just held it between myself and this man. I wasn't about to have him pin me against the wall. I watched his hands and feet as he kept babbling. Finally I pointed my nightstick at him and poked him slightly in the ribs. "Now look, quit moving in on me. You stand and talk from *there*." Because I was tired of all the footwork.

But he didn't seem able to keep his distance. He kept "getting up in my face." Well, I had already separated him from the people who had called for help, and now it occurred to me that one way to get him out of the building was to take advantage of his peculiar habit. "Come on, let's go downstairs and talk some more." I headed for the stairs and sure enough, he stayed right with me. I hadn't gone down more than a couple of steps when the officers who had gotten the run came dashing up.

"You got a burglary in progress here?"

I shook my head and as the three of us walked the man out, I explained as much as I knew and turned him over to them. I was glad to be rid of him. I was also a little disappointed not to have gotten a real "in progress."

There have been many studies about why people become police officers: because they want to boss people, or help people; because it's a steady job with good benefits and retirement pay after twenty years; and on and on. Yet I think that most police end up wanting to be a hero. I certainly did. There was no question that I wanted to live, but I guess every police officer longs to have a really close call where he stops a crime or catches a criminal in the act or masters a dangerous scene and everything is beautiful.

With many people on the streets during the summer, it became particularly clear that both my own self-consciousness and the attention I received from citizens had diminished over the period I had been on patrol. I no longer felt conspicuous. I had simply grown accustomed to my uniform and my work.

The public's reaction to me as a female officer had originally been mixed. Friendly greetings, waves, comments of "Right on, sister," and peace signs; and sneers, yells of "whore," "dike," and so on. Depending on my mood, sometimes the attention had been exciting and at other times it had been a burden that wore me out. Now, seeing uniformed women on patrol no longer surprised most people in D.C. Women numbered about 260, or 6 times the figure for 1968, when I had joined the force. I drew little more notice than any male police. There were, however, occasional comments about my stripes—I was the only female sergeant in Three D —and my gun.

Several cynical street dudes snickered that I got my stripes because I was white or because I slept with the right people. I supposed they were trying to rationalize the fact that women were first seen in uniform in 1972 and now one of them had already been promoted faster than any male who had joined the force that same year. To those who seemed interested in the facts, I explained that the majority of female officials were actually black, and that policewomen had been around in plainclothes since 1917. I added that I had been in police work since 1968, had studied hard for the sergeant's exam, and that many men who had joined back then had been promoted in less time than me. I didn't bother to argue with those who maintained flatly that it just wasn't right for a woman to be a sergeant when there were men available.

The gun seemed to be the last aspect about me that people could accept. Apparently there were still many citizens who just couldn't conceive of a woman carrying, much less using, one. I answered a call for a "woman firing a shotgun at people in the twenty-two hundred block of Twelfth Place, Northwest." I drew my revolver before running into the block. As I ran, the crowds on the sidewalks shouted, "Look, she's got a gun." "She's got a gun in her hand." "Hey, lady, you'd better put that away unless you know how to use it." Male officers with guns in their hands were not drawing such comments. I felt I couldn't have gotten more attention had I been running naked through this crowded block. Once I learned that the automatic rifle (not a shotgun, after all) had been seized and the shooting was over (two to the hospital), I holstered my weapon. As I returned to my cruiser later, the crowd spotted me again and, not seeing the gun in my hand, shouted, "She's dropped it!" "She doesn't have her gun." "It's lost." All this concern.

August started hot and steamy. I had just returned from a leave I had requested in order to take a crash course in preparation for the bar exam, which had been given the last two days of July.

I cruised along Fourteenth Street, noting the diminished action. While I had been home studying, Inspector Crooke, the new Third District Commander, had set up a special plainclothes detail of twenty-four female officers to break up the prostitution traffic and related crime on the Strip. The women had been given a day's training in terminology and the elements required for a valid arrest under the solicitation law. They could not initiate advances or do certain other things which amounted to "entrapment." The customer had to mention both the product and the price.

Inadvertently, the female police officers in civilian dress, with their service revolvers and radios concealed under their clothes or in their pocketbooks, turned out to have more appeal than the pros. They made hundreds of arrests and totally disrupted the business of the pimps and prostitutes. The five-week operation which was about to conclude had been an immense success. The Strip had lost its prominence as one of the wide-open red-light districts in the country.

I had mixed feelings about having missed out on the action. In one sense I was jealous because it was an exciting detail with opportunities for testing women as police officers in a way I had never experienced. Yet I was glad not to have been confronted with the dilemmas of vice enforcement—the area of law enforcement I liked the least, because there were no innocent victims to protect, and because the public seemed indifferent.

As I swung off Fourteenth Street onto Thomas Circle, I passed a tall, slender figure in silver high-heeled boots, silver lamé pants and a silver halter top. I recognized him as one of the regular homosexuals who hung out in the area.

Farther along I spotted a clearly suspicious group. Two white marines with crew cuts were lounging against a stone wall being talked to by a couple of black dudes in fancy clothes. A white man on Fourteenth Street was likely not to know his way around. Furthermore, a lot of servicemen came to D.C. and really got taken by local racketeers. I passed the four men, looking them over carefully. On the midnight tour you search for things to do and have time to check out any activity or person that looks questionable.

I reached for my microphone. At the far end of Thomas Circle I saw a scout car I had already passed once coming toward me. Then I heard it on the radio. "Scout one-oh-one. Four suspicious subjects on Thomas Circle. Two Negro males and two white males who are marines. We have reason to believe it's a Murphy game. Hold us to counsel them."

A Murphy game is a confidence trick. It can work in numerous ways. One version might involve two con men inviting two straight guys for a good time and some girls. When they arrive at an address, they show concern and warn the straight guys to take precautions against being rolled. They may suggest that the two marks put their money, watches and other valuables into an envelope one of them can hang onto. So the straight guys aren't even asked to trust their newfound buddies. But the envelope supposedly containing the valuables is never actually given to either of the marks. A switch takes place and a similar envelope stuffed with news-paper is all the straight guys find when they get around to opening it sometime later. The confidence men are long gone.

I moved my car closer to the group on Thomas Circle and watched as two officers walked up to the four men. One stayed a small distance back; the other started conversing. A moment later the group was cracking up—going through antics that could only be interpreted as hilarity.

The two officers retreated quickly and came to the window of my car. For a minute they were speechless. Then one of them said, "Jesus Christ, Sarge, we had *four marine buddies* over there and I never felt like such an asshole in my life!"

It turned out that the two black men were *from* Washington, showing their friends around the city.

"It sure *looked* bad," I said. "I was just about to get on the radio myself—"

"You don't know how bad it was," said the first officer. "The two black guys had just finished giving their buddies a tour of the Strip and telling them what kinds of things went on so they wouldn't get taken. After *we* finished talking to them, one of the black guys said, 'Oh yeah, we forgot to warn you about the dangers of the D.C. Po'lice.'"

On Thursday, August 8, 1974, I worked the 1500 to 2300 shift and on a TV set at Three D watched President Nixon announce that he would resign. During the tour there were many calls for police assistance with crowds in front of 1600 Pennsylvania Avenue. *The Washington Post*, at Fifteenth and L streets, Northwest, received numerous bomb threats throughout the evening. On my way home, I stopped at the Greyhound Bus Station and picked up an early edition of Friday's paper. I had been on the spot when an event of national importance took place.

Although my activities were seldom affected directly because I happened to work in D.C., I always had an underlying awareness of being in the nation's capital. Having the White House located in Second District meant I heard radio calls which involved the police in addition to the White House's own Executive Protective Service. Gary and I lived in a house eight blocks east of the Capitol Building. I walked or rode my bike through the Capitol grounds to get to law school. I think other residents of Washington, and tourists, too, have a sense of immediacy with their nation while they are here.

I had come to expect myself to react in a purely professional way to any police scene.

A run came out, "Scout one hundred and any official, a shooting inside the Emerson Market, twelve-oh-nine Thirteenth Street, Northwest." Scout 100 responded 10-4 (two-man unit), and I radioed "Cruiser two-four-two responding." I was just around the corner and first to arrive.

Delivery trucks and cars were double-parked in front of the store. The front door was closed. I ran up, opened the door and saw a body lying across my path, bleeding from the right side of his head. One of several people standing around told me he had been shot. "If he was shot in the head," I thought, "why is he conscious and still looking at me?" Later I learned that the blood I saw on his head was from a pistol whipping. He had also been shot once in the stomach, the bullet coming out at his shoulder.

I ran out to my car, verified that an ambulance was on the way and dashed back into the store. I heard the ambulance arrive as I started getting a tentative description of the assailant. Ambulance crews in Washington respond so quickly that police seldom have to use their first aid training. I had decided against questioning the victim on the floor since he was obviously in bad shape and suffering. The checkout clerk said she had been robbed by the assailant, who had then shot the victim, a deliveryman from Ottenberg's Bakery, when he had tried to stop the holdup. An officer from 100 Scout arrived and took the lookout while I returned to my cruiser to call for additional units—Mobile Crime Laboratory, Homicide detectives, Robbery detectives.

Later in the day I read and signed the report on the crime.

People often asked me how I reacted to scenes where someone had been seriously injured. My response to the Emerson Market shooting was typical. While I'm present, I have no time or inclination to become emotionally involved. The thoughts racing through my mind are of procedures and duties and what to do first. Whom must I notify? Where's a rope to rope off the area? Which witness has the best information so I can get a tentative lookout on the air fastest?

A couple of days after the shooting, I was stopped at a red light next to another Ottenberg Bakery delivery truck. When I looked at the driver and realized his colleague was lying in a hospital bed, the offense finally struck me as a human tragedy and not just a complicated radio run. I called out to the driver, "How is Mr. Keenan doing?"

He answered, "He's going to make it. They took him out of intensive care yesterday."

As he drove off I actually had tears in my eyes—two days after the event.

20

GAIL COBB

I was working a Saturday in September. It had rained all morning and then turned warm and humid. I felt I was going to have a busy evening shift.

One of my cars got a call for the rear of an address in the 1300 block of Clifton, Northwest. Disorderly kids. I decided to ride up because I wanted to talk to the officer about his missing Reserve meeting, for which I had to write him an excuse.

As I turned onto Clifton from Fourteenth, a young woman ran toward me, frantically waving her arms and screaming, "Stop that man. Don't let him take my children."

The radio was buzzing with someone else's message so I jumped out of my car without telling the dispatcher where I was or asking for backup. The woman pointed out a large but calm-looking man standing in the street next to the driver's side of a car parked at the curb. Another woman, who turned out to be the first one's sister, was screaming incoherently behind the man. I approached. Two young children, about one and three years old, were inside the car.

The man said he was the children's father. He and their mother didn't live together, and he was taking them with him because the mother didn't take proper care of them. He

said the police had visited their apartment the night before
and agreed that he should have the children because his wife
used drugs.

"Do you have a court custody order?" I asked.

"No. Maybe I can get one Monday. But she can't have
the kids now because she wants to take them to Virginia, and
I'll never get them back."

The woman said her mother was arriving shortly from
Virginia and yes, she did want to take the kids home with her
mother then.

As we talked, I had placed myself at the door of the car
between mother and father. I shifted my body frequently to
keep the mother away from the father and both of them away
from the door. The sister screamed that I better give the
children to their mother or she would fight, and she started
picking up bottles, brandishing them and smashing them on
the sidewalk.

A crowd was gathering.

I was stalling, trying to think of a solution for these
parents. First I pleaded with the mother to give in and let
the father have the kids. She screamed and threatened, and
her sister's agitation grew worse. Then I pleaded with the
father to let the mother take the children. He calmly explained that she would go to Virginia and never return.

"Well, you're going to have to reach some agreement
because we [the royal police we although I was alone] cannot
let you fight in the street."

Someone in the crowd must have put in a 10-33 (police-
officer-in-trouble call) because at that point, a scout car came
racing, siren blaring, into the block. I appreciated the backup
but hoped the additional officers wouldn't irritate the crowd.
They didn't. They were beautiful. First they held back, just
watching and letting me continue to talk while they got the

gist of things. Then one officer walked up to me and quietly suggested the solution. Give one child to the mother and one to the father. Of course. I should have thought of it. I made the proposal and the couple agreed. The mother took the one-year-old and walked off. The father drove away with the three-year-old. The crowd dispersed, and I returned to my car and drove north on Fourteenth Street.

Three blocks away, I saw a body fly across the street and land between two parked cars. Then four or five men jumped on him. A bystander yelled that one of the men had a gun. I shouted my location into the radio as an emergency and jumped out of the car, hand on gun. Spectators were shouting. I hesitated before piling into the mess because I was confused. The man on the bottom of the pile was not being beaten. The others seemed to be just holding him down. I couldn't imagine whether he was a thug being disarmed by good citizens or what.

Then the man on top of the pile lifted his head to tell me everything was okay, and I recognized him as a plainclothes sergeant from Vice Squad. Sirens were blaring by now as my "assistance" started arriving on the scene. Humiliated, I dashed back to my car and radioed, "Have all units disregard emergency at Fourteenth and Fairmont. Everything is under control. Vice has an arrest. We need one transport. Put all other units back in service."

I had never before been the object of a police-in-trouble call, and that night I had two, neither of which amounted to anything.

Friday morning, September 20, I was doing chores around the house and thinking about a lecture I had to give the following Tuesday at the FBI Academy at Quantico. Police administrators would be coming from cities throughout the country for a week of management training.

I had spoken to similar groups before. As usual, my topic was women in law enforcement. By now, the speech was fairly standard and would need only some updating and minor changes. But once again I had a premonition of the misgivings I would feel when I delivered it. In a sense I had lived through and been instrumental in the change that had come about on the D.C. force. But as a spokeswoman for the movement to get other women on patrol and persuade police managers to accept the idea, I found my audiences often expected me to be more than I was. They wanted me to give firsthand accounts of how I personally had done every police stunt or duty that they had ever heard of. Women's experience in police work was extensive enough by now so that for every police task, one could find a woman who had performed it. Yet I was obviously only one person, with my own set of strengths and weaknesses, just completing my second year of patrol. In actuality, there were many police experiences I had never had. Nor had any other single officer, even with five years of experience. But I still felt the tension between my role as an individual and as a "representative."

Around noon, the telephone rang. I picked it up and said hello.

"Mary Ellen? I'm glad you're home." It was a friend of Gary's and mine.

"Yeah, I don't go to work until this afternoon. Why? What's up?"

"You haven't heard."

I said I didn't know what he was talking about. And then he told me. He had heard a radio bulletin stating only that a female patrol officer in downtown Washington had just been shot to death.

As soon as he hung up, I called Police Communications, identified myself and asked if they could tell me the name of the officer who had been killed. Her name was Gail Cobb. But I was told not to say anything to the press because they hadn't yet notified all the relatives.

I put down the phone. I had not known Gail Cobb. In another sense she had been my sister. Suddenly I thought of Gary, who was out of town on a special assignment. I was afraid he might hear a newsflash that didn't carry the dead woman's name. As it turned out, the first release Gary heard did identify the officer, so he never had a moment of concern about me.

I switched on the radio, and after a while more news came out. Gail A. Cobb, a first-year Metropolitan Police officer, had been shot to death in an underground garage at Twentieth and L streets, Northwest. Officer Cobb was twenty-four years old. She had been walking her beat when a civilian told her a man with a gun had just run into an underground garage nearby. Officer Cobb ran into the garage and stopped a man in a business suit who was coming out of a restroom. As she put him up against the wall to frisk him, he drew a gun, whirled and shot her before she could draw her own service revolver. Officer Cobb never learned that this man was a robbery suspect who, with an accomplice, had already fired on two other officers. He had evidently gone into the restroom to change clothes or disguise his appearance. Shortly after the slaying, the police arrested a man and charged him with homicide. A second suspect was still being sought. Gail Cobb was the first American policewoman killed in the line of duty since the FBI began keeping statistics in 1960.

By the time I reported to work Friday night, more and more details were coming out. Both of Gail Cobb's parents were in fields related to law enforcement. Her father was a senior captain of the guards at the Lorton correctional facility. Her mother was a school crossing guard. The bullet that had killed Gail Cobb had gone through her arm and into her heart. She was survived by a young child.

It was the custom in the department from the time a police officer was killed until the funeral took place for all officers and officials on the force to wear a strip of black electrical tape across their badges as a sign of mourning. At work that night, an officer found some tape and went around taping everybody's badge.

A tremendous unity of feeling and purpose arises among police officers when one of them is killed. Above and beyond this, one could sense a kind of sisterhood among the women. It wasn't anything clannish. Even the men would turn to the female officers with a kind of unspoken sympathy and the thought that this was really something for them. As I was leaving the scene of a false gun-call that Friday night, an SOD (Special Operations Division) officer who was on tactical patrol in Third District put on his red light and spotlight to pull me over. He walked up to my car and silently handed me a photograph of the second robbery suspect, who was still out and wanted. It was significant that he had pulled *me* over, because there were other Third District vehicles all around. I'm sure he just thought, "She's a woman. She's going to want to get this guy a little more than everybody else." As he left, he said, "You might want to show this to the people in Third District."

Saturday night, the second robbery suspect turned himself in.

*   *   *

Gail Cobb's funeral was scheduled for Tuesday morning, September 24. In the afternoon of the same day, I was going to speak to the police administrators. Monday night, I reviewed and made some additions to my standard talk.

First facts. "In January, 1972, Washington, D.C., began using women on patrol and assigning female patrol supervisors. Thus we became one of the first departments to employ significant numbers of women in these duties. By summer of 1972, eighty female patrol officers and eighty new male patrol officers were made the objects of a detailed performance evaluation study conducted by the Urban Institute, with Police Foundation funds. Many veteran police held their breath, convinced that the women-on-patrol experiment would be a short-lived tragedy. Either a woman would shoot and kill an attacker whom a hypothetical male officer could have subdued without a gun; or a woman would be killed in a situation where a hypothetical male would not. Either way, the incident would mark the end of women on patrol.

"That was two years ago. Women are now an integral part of the patrol force and every other division of the department. . . . Contrary to critics' fears, D.C. and the nation made it through the first day, the first month, year, even the first two years of having women in the front lines before any woman had to pay the ultimate price of having patrol work open to her. When Gail Cobb was shot to death last Friday, the department's program of women on patrol was two years and eight months old, although Gail Cobb herself was only a rookie with five months of street experience. Gail Cobb was shot when a man she was investigating spun around and fired before she had drawn her revolver. In July this year, another female patrol officer shot and killed a man she was confronting on a bus when he suddenly reached into his pocket. She thought he had a gun. He did not. He had a small knife and a piece of lead pipe. He also had a long police record including assault with a deadly weapon and assault with intent to rape. These are the life-and-death encounters which men have had to deal with for years. Women now share them for keeps. They have paid their dues as patrol officers, and they will stay.

"I do think Gail Cobb's death will have an important impact on women-on-patrol programs across the country. The death should have a sobering influence on any woman who was attracted to the job by flashy publicity and glamour. It should have a sobering influence on any police recruiters who were more interested in a female applicant's face and figure than her stamina and street savvy. It should have a sobering influence on police administrators who thrust untrained women into street patrol hoping to see them fail. It should have a sobering influence on police academy instructors who allowed squeamish women to slip through firearms or self-defense training without adequate demonstrations of skill. It should have a sobering influence on any senior patrol officers who treated rookie policewomen as a joke and did not give them the benefit of their experience.

"Let me change the subject now and report on the findings of the researchers' study of women on patrol in Washington. . . .

"First, sick leave. It was found that women did not use or abuse their sick leave any more or less than men. Women were not injured more than men.

"Women did not resign or get fired more often than men.

"Women responded to the same types of calls as men. No difference was found in the ability of men and women to handle violent and potentially violent situations.

"In overall performance ratings by supervisors, men and women came out about the same, with the vast majority of both being found satisfactory. These ratings are curious, because most of the supervisors still express the opinion that in general, women do not make good patrol officers. However, when it came time to rate officers individually, they apparently could not substantiate their general opinions.

"I have given you some of the findings that reflect well on women, but I am not trying to hide the problems. The two most serious encountered were on the one hand, overprotectiveness and stereotyping of women by men; and on the other hand, lack of both aggressiveness and confidence of women. The overprotectiveness took many forms. In the beginning of the program, there was outright sabotage of the policy of equal treatment. . . .

"The other side of the problem—that women on patrol were not as aggressive in initiating enforcement action as were the men—was substantiated by statistics showing that 80 percent of the new women made fewer arrests and fewer traffic stops than did the comparison men.

"Time and experience seem to be helping solve both these problems. Significant strides were made this summer in improving the confidence and initiative of twenty-four of D.C.'s policewomen, who were given plainclothes detail to try to reduce prostitution and related street crime which had taken over a strip along Fourteenth Street. Uniformed patrols were not accomplishing enough. . . . The results were remarkable both in the reduction of offenses and the newfound aggressiveness of the women. Department statistics show that July's prostitution-related crime was cut in half over the previous year. I have proof even more reliable than department statistics. The manager of the all-night drugstore in the area told me that sales of prophylactics went so far down in July that the store was overstocked and did not have to order any for August.

"It is the change in the women, however, that interests me and is relevant to this talk. Women who previously allowed male partners to take over on patrol now had only female partners. All month long they had to fight for themselves. They did, and won. They made 516 arrests—mostly men—for crimes ranging from disorderly conduct and soliciting for prostitution to assault and carrying dangerous weapons. The detail was so successful that eight of the women will continue to work together on a permanent basis, and new women may be sent to them for training.

"I find the success of the detail ironic. One of the principles at the heart of the early movement to put women on patrol was the integration of men and women throughout the department. Old segregated women's bureaus were to be abolished. I still think that complete segregation is poor management. But this summer's experience convinces me that there ought to be occasions when women are forced to rely on themselves and each other, or neither they nor the men around them will get over the problems of the male over-protectiveness and the female underaggressiveness with which our culture has burdened us.

"For the benefit of any of you who come from departments that do not yet employ women for all police duties, I want to make some recommendations about how to begin. But first we will break. . . ."

Tuesday, the twenty-fourth, was an unseasonably cold, sunlit September day. I put on my uniform and walked to the bus stop. It was 8 A.M. I would join at the D.C. Armory with police from all the districts and units in Washington, as well as delegations from other departments around the country.

A car with New Jersey tags, full of police, stopped and asked me for directions.

"Oh, is the funeral today?" asked a citizen also waiting for the bus. *The* funeral. Follow-up stories had been in the papers and on the news since Friday.

A bus was coming when another car with some D.C. police I didn't know stopped and gave me a lift.

The huge Armory parking lot filled rapidly with busloads of officers and cars from Delaware, Virginia, Connecticut, New York, New Jersey and elsewhere. Among visiting officials was Inspector Gertrude Schimmel of New York City, the nation's highest ranking woman in law enforcement. Special Operations Division had set up a registration table at which out-of-town people signed in, stated how many vehicles they had for the procession to the cemetery, and got general instructions. I saw arm insignia marked Cleveland, Chicago and Detroit. A call went out for additional black tape for shrouding of badges.

Despite the tragedy underlying the occasion, the atmosphere at the Armory and during the walk to Holy Comforter Catholic Church was not somber. There was the camaraderie and reunion of people who in some cases hadn't seen each other for a long time. Police exchanged gossip and news. A woman I had known from Personnel came over and said she had heard rumors that I had resigned and gone with the U.S. Attorney's Office. "No, I'm still on the department." My prospective job was half a year away. I was trying to keep it quiet at least until December, when I would know definitely whether I had passed the bar.

When we formed by districts and walked in a long double

line to the church, there was clowning about who wanted to be partners with whom, and speculation on the number of people showing up. Official observers were already estimating that this was the largest turnout of law enforcement officers—over two thousand—at any police funeral in the city's history.

The block in front of the church had been closed to non-police traffic. "EMERGENCY NO PARKING" signs were taped to the trees along both sides of the street. Hundreds of citizens sat on the stoops and stone walls of the row houses opposite the church. Our own formation of twos became rows of about six deep, filling the street. Delegations filed in to view the body. As the police from other cities paraded by, we all commented on their uniforms and appearance. Males whistled at female officers. The honor guard with flags paraded up and down several times. The mood was still not morbid. There were many cameras outside. None were being allowed in the church. Then my group went in to walk by the coffin.

The nine hundred seats in the church were filled. About three-quarters of them appeared to hold uniformed officers. Gail Cobb was lying in an open casket, dressed in a kelly-green suit and slightly made up. She looked pretty, petite and very young. She was wearing gold hoop earrings that she could not have worn on duty.

We went down one aisle, past the coffin, and up the other aisle out of the church to take our places in the street again. The day was still unusually cold, and many of us shivered.

Within the church the service started. The Reverend R. Joseph Dooley, chaplain or the Catholic Police and Firemen Society, preached the homily. We listened over loudspeakers set outside.

"Police families know that this moment may come at any time. The physical risk of being a police officer is great. The tragic silence that follows the reading of a fellow officer's name at roll call tears the very fabric of our country. . . .

"Today the rows and rows of blue, of green, of brown, of gray—the rows of brother officers, sad of heart, come here because they share in your loss.

"Gail Cobb was vivacious, warm, friendly, fun-loving—and industrious. Her goals in life were set. . . .

"Something happened last Friday that changed the course of history not only for Gail's family and loved ones but for the law enforcement community. As the first policewoman in the nation to give her life in the line of duty, it is now an established fact that the criminal makes no distinction between the sexes. A police officer is a police officer, regardless. It is your badge and the blue of your uniform that makes the difference."

Outside we could hear dogs barking. An airplane flew overhead. The ranks were quiet.

"Ninety-one other officers throughout the country have given their lives already this year, and God only knows how many innocent civilians have been slain. We must all do our part to prevent this tragic toll from happening. Today we will take Gail to her final resting place. But it is imperative that we bury only her body, not her spirit.

"Pray for her and her loved ones who have suffered this loss. Pray that God will find her worthy of the reward for which she lived and worked and prayed. May her soul and the souls of all her brother officers who have given their lives rest in peace. Amen."

Communion was given.

I wasn't really thinking "what if it had been me" because that would have been simply an end. I thought of what I would be feeling and doing if it had been Gary. The thought also kept going through my mind that it had been inevitable that eventually a female officer would be killed, and I was at least glad that she was killed honorably. She wasn't doing anything stupid. Her life had not been wasted in an accidental death. There could have been mistakes that would have been so much harder to live with.

Gail Cobb didn't have her gun out, and quietly there had been talk about that. If she had lived, or if she had had a partner killed while she hadn't drawn her weapon, the talk would have been more open. But it was too easy and un-fitting to second-guess the dead.

As I looked at the other women, I thought that in a sense we almost needed this tragedy to mark the fact that our work was for real. It was too easy to take the job lightly. I didn't know what things were like the first time a black police officer was killed in D.C., but I felt there might have been a similarity. This being a predominantly black city, there may have been a lot of black cops who believed they would be treated differently, or their time might not come—that somehow it wasn't as dangerous for them as for a white cop. Many of us women must have felt that same way. We always knew someone could gun us down, but at the same time, we def-initely experienced a different kind of treatment by less serious criminals. Now the point was driven home. When it really counted, there would be no distinctions made because of sex.

The church organist played the "Battle Hymn of the Republic" and almost everybody outside sang. It was a song most people knew, and we needed to do something at that point. The voices were particularly strong on the chorus.

The hearse maneuvered into position and the doors at the top of the church steps opened. The ranks outside broke as some officers got ready to join the procession to the cemetery while others prepared to go on duty, return home, or do other things.

I chatted with some women officers from New York and then started walking home to get my car and drive out to the FBI Academy.

On my way I came across a citizen with his car backed out of a private driveway and stalled in the street, blocking the entire lane of traffic. Automobiles were honking. I stopped. "What's the problem?"

"I don't know. It just conked out."

"Well, let's push it back into the driveway so traffic can get by."

I leaned into one rear fender while he pushed on the other. The street and driveway were level and the car started moving. Suddenly we realized someone better get in and steer, and since the guy was on the left-hand fender, he ran forward and jumped into the driver's seat. I pushed a little more and we got the car parked in the driveway. It occurred to me that he had made no comment nor batted an eyelash at my doing the pushing. The memory of Youth Division days when we used to ask male officers at the stations to gas our cars flashed through my mind. In so many ways the role of women was different now.

"Thanks a lot," said the car's owner.

"You're welcome." The exercise had warmed me up. I pulled down my jacket and started walking away.

"Hey," the man called after me. "Hey, Sarge, take care."

I raised my hand in acknowledgment and kept going.